Shamanism: An A–Z Reference Guide

SHAMANISM

AN A-Z REFERENCE GUIDE

Beliefs and Practices from
Around the World

MARILYN WALKER, PhD

Interior and Cover Designer: Francesca Pacchini
Art Producer: Janice Ackerman
Editor: Samantha Barbaro

ISBN: Print   978-1-64611-204-3
      eBook   978-1-64611-205-0
      R0

WITH THANKS TO THE COUNTLESS INDIGENOUS PEOPLE, many of them shamans, who taught me so much, among them Anai, Chulu, Bair Rinchinov, Mosesee Audlakiak, Matilde and Bernie Sulurayok, Emile Gautreau, Jeorgina Larocque, Bokova, Bob Sam—I wish I could name you all. To Skip Koolage, Michael Harner, Mihály Hoppál, and Bill Fitzhugh for the opportunities you made available in Indigenous and shamanic studies. And to my father, Peter Walker, who taught me from a very young age to see things with an open mind and open heart.

In the midst of such a fit of mysterious and overwhelming delight I became a Shaman, not knowing myself how it came about . . . I could see and hear in a totally different way. I had gained my 'quamaneq,' my enlightenment, the shaman-light of brain and body, and this in such a manner that it was not only I who could see through the darkness of life, but the same bright light also shone out from me, imperceptible to human beings but visible to all spirits of earth and sky and sea, and these now came to me and became my helping spirits."

—Iglulik shaman of the Canadian Arctic, Aua, in the 1920s

CONTENTS

INTRODUCTION

I'm a retired academic who spent most of my career living and working in Indigenous cultures—in the Canadian North, Siberia, Mongolia, India, Southeast Asia, and the Bön Po Indigenous tradition of Tibet, as well as other parts of the world where shamans are still practicing. I had so many life-changing experiences that can only be touched on for a book of this kind. I decided to write this book because, even among my university colleagues and closest friends, there is so much prejudice and misunderstanding about what shamanism is and why it is relevant today. Although much has changed in the more than 50 or so years since I first started working in Indigenous communities, misunderstanding and prejudice remain.

"Shamanism" was a Tungusic Siberian word used to describe their spiritual leaders. The term was later adopted by Western anthropologists as a way to classify and name the "Other." Today it functions as an umbrella term for a broad range of Indigenous spiritual practices across time, continents, and cultures, used by anthropologists and sometimes by Indigenous People themselves.

This book addresses the diversity of shamanic traditions temporally and geographically; as well, it identifies core elements of a pan-shamanic complex that spans time and space, going back to the origins of humanity. It would take volumes, and has done so, to acknowledge the global scope of shamanist traditions, so I have chosen topics and cultures that represent both diversity and shared beliefs and practices. Our learning, especially about such topics as this one, is never-ending. One can talk in generalities but not in absolutes—there are many controversies in the study of shamanism, even among shamans themselves.

It is a difficult task as an anthropologist to portray other cultures and traditions for the general reader! How to honor local norms and values while respecting all traditions in this great human experience? I remember being a young researcher working in the Canadian Arctic and asking about Inuit traditions. Although I was treated kindly—as Inuit treat a child, since Inuit said I had to learn as a child learns, supported and guided by teachers and friends—I started to feel uncomfortable as a Southern, white *kabloona* (a non-Inuit), and so I expressed my misgivings to an Inuk elder one day. He said, "You have to tell your people what it is like here." Not everyone could visit the places I had, but I could act as a sort of translator between cultures.

The ancestry of all humanity is shamanist, though many of us have moved away from it, even dismissed it as irrelevant to the modern day. But we need these ways more than ever before. The shamanic worldway is ecological in the broadest sense: It is grounded in a moral and ethical relationship between humans and the natural world and between this physical world and the metaphysical realm—human and nonhuman. The distinctions on which science is based (man/nature, mind/body) are connections (mind, body, spirit, emotions) in the shamanic worldway. Whereas science's capacity for dividing up the physical world into species, elements, or parts of the body is well recognized, the more metaphorical shamanic way recognizes infinitely expanding connection as the basis of the universe and of universal knowledge.

Shamanist traditions invoke the spirit world of Non-Ordinary Reality to assist in the problems and dilemmas of this physical world of Ordinary Reality.

Shamans are adept at mediating these realms, but anyone, shaman or not, may ask for spirit guidance directly and may regularly interact with the spirit world. Such traditions, which are undergoing a revival after centuries and even millennia of suppression, are being explored with a great deal of interest by Indigenous Peoples themselves—for example, the shared visits between the Squamish Nation of British Columbia and the Bön Monastery of Menri in northern India or the Russian and Chinese conferences of the past few years in which shamans participate along with social scientists, physicists, parapsychologists, mathematicians, artists, and musicians, among others.

With an exploding literature on shamanism—much written by shamans themselves—and a major paradigm shift away from the scientific faith that spirits do not exist, we no longer debate the existence of the spirit world; instead, we access, navigate, and describe it.[1] Shamanism can expand our understanding of the human mind and its seemingly limitless potential. It points us, especially those of us constrained by the limitations of organized religions, conventional science, and conventional medicine, to consider the nature of reality itself.

I started out as a student of shamanism and now teach workshops and courses, and offer individual consultations that draw on my personal and academic explorations but also respect the intellectual property rights of my teachers. Bob Sam, a Tlingit medicine man in Southeast Alaska, told me stories: Some, he said, you can relate to your students, some can be written down, and some are private and only for you to hear and act on. I was taught to connect with my own spirit teachers and to navigate my own way in the spirit world. I am amazed at what comes to me from my spirit teachers; as I say to my students, I don't have that much imagination to be making these things up! And I am gratified at how what comes not *from* me but *through* me to provide hope and guidance for so many people who struggle with today's problems; they say they are helped on their life's journey by these ways of being when more conventional methods do not help.

The book is not meant to be read cover to cover, nor is it meant to teach rituals or shamanic healing techniques. Instead, it will assist the lay reader in understanding Indigenous spirituality and show how the lessons not only have relevance to the modern world but may be what we need to save it from the destructive path humanity is now on. Material wealth pales in contrast to the richness of life that comes from living in partnership with the world of spirits.

There is a role for all of us to play in this global renaissance, whether we are Indigenous or not. We can support organizations such as the Foundation for Shamanic Studies with its Living Treasures of Shamanism and Indigenous Assistance program. We can recognize and honor intellectual property rights of Indigenous Peoples and of shamans especially, and advocate with religious and humanitarian groups to be more inclusive and to make amends for the past. And we can blend the New Age spirituality of the West, with its interest in personal growth and transformation, with the traditional role of the shaman for the benefit of all beings.

ALLIES, SPIRIT

A SHAMAN'S SPIRIT helpers may be called allies, helping spirits, guardian spirits, familiar spirits, or familiars.

SEE ALSO: **SPIRITS**

ALTARS

ALTARS ARE PLACES, either inside a home or outside in nature, where spirits can be contacted for help and rituals conducted to show respect. Spirits may even reside there or in items placed there as power objects. They may be personal for any member of a culture or the prerogative of a shaman.

Hmong shaman at her altar, northern Thailand, 1999. The shaman's bench is what the shaman "rides" when in trance and so is the equivalent, as the Hmong are horticulturalists, of the Central Asian "ride" of the horse.

Hmong shaman's altar (detail) showing Buddhist and Chinese influence in the gold and silver paper, paper cutouts, stick incense, and porcelain cups, 1999.

A SHAMAN MOVES between an everyday state of consciousness and an altered state of consciousness (ASC), between an Ordinary State of Consciousness (OSC) and a Shamanic State of Consciousness (SSC), or between Ordinary Reality (OR) and Non-Ordinary Reality (NOR). An ASC is achieved via the shamanic journey, which is generally accepted as the defining characteristic of shamanism. Some shamans journey in a deep trance, unaware of this reality for the time they are journeying; others experience both states simultaneously. Either way, a shaman must be competent in both OR and NOR.

To induce an ASC, various techniques are used cross-culturally from chanting and singing to the use of instruments such as the drum, rattle, gong, or mouth harp. Dance, sleep deprivation or immersion in darkness, fasting and dehydration, isolation and austerities, and cleansing and purifying rites such as smudging with plants are utilized. In some cultures, drugs are used.

Shamans explain addictions, depression, and other conditions that modern medicine defines as medical problems as resulting from someone getting lost in NOR and being unable to find their way back to OR. Getting stuck in the other world or leaving a soul part there results from inexperience, ignorance, or lack of preparation and guidance. For people who cannot accept the *reality* of NOR or SSC, Michael Harner uses the term "cognicentrism," which is the consciousness equivalent of ethnocentrism.[2]

Altered State of Consciousness (ASC)
Ordinary State of Consciousness (OSC)
Shamanic State of Consciousness (SSC)
Ordinary Reality (OR)
Non-Ordinary Reality (NOR)

SEE ALSO: **DANCE, MOVEMENT; MOUTH HARP, JEW'S HARP, JAW HARP; SMOKE, INCENSE, SMUDGE**

AMULET

THE TERM REFERS to an object that magically (rather that physically) protects the owner. Amulets tend to be found objects such as stones, pieces of bone, animal claws, feathers, or bits of a plant that a person carries with them to ward off negative influences, but they may also be beads, medallions, or other such objects meaningful to the wearer. Amulets may be worn on a necklace, carried in a medicine pouch or a pocket, or sewn into the hem of a coat or dress. One might be placed over a doorway to stop evil spirits from entering or be infused in water to wash down a boat before venturing out to sea. As part of their doctoring, shamans might give a curing amulet to a patient, but anyone might find or be guided by the spirits to find their own.

Knud Rasmussen (1930) writing about the amulets of the Padlermiut (Caribou Eskimo of Hudson's Bay):

 The child must have its amulets as quickly as possible after birth. These amulets, if they are animals, must be caught alive without first being wounded, or, if they are flowers, they must not be plucked by the father or the mother but only bought by them and preferably of people from distant villages. Later, the wearer of the amulet must never kill any of the animals of which his or her amulet is made, otherwise it will lose its power."[3]

SEE ALSO: **FETISH; TALISMAN**

ANCESTORS

IN MANY SHAMANIC traditions, ancestors are the most powerful helping spirits of the shaman—their personalities or characteristics blend with those of the shaman to amplify the shaman's power. A shaman can heal ancestral trauma that is transgenerational and the cause of afflictions in this life—when a shaman travels back in time to heal an ancestor, the carrier of that trauma in this life will also be healed. And vice versa—when a shaman heals someone in this life, they can also heal the family line and the trauma will not be passed down to descendants.

Shamans may come from an ancestral line of shamans, whereas neoshamans may not know their shamanic lineage or may not have inherited it for some reason; thus, they will rely on other spirit helpers.

ANIMAL LANGUAGE

MANY INDIGENOUS CULTURES tell of people who can communicate with animals. Hunters may ask an animal to show itself so that it may be killed in a respectful way to provide for the hunter's family. Others may talk to an animal who is threatening a community to ask it to go away, as one Inuk is able to do with polar bears. Animal language may be a direct connection to Spirit; as the Mongolian shaman Maamaa described it, "Cuckoo is my interpreter. I need to use Cuckoo when talking to my *Ongod*/Spirit."

ANIMALS

IN SOME INDIGENOUS cultures, animals, like humans, have souls or spirits. In many Indigenous cultures, animals are equals to humans and sometimes are superior. They have qualities that humans don't have and may be called upon for those very qualities. A particular animal may become a familiar or guardian spirit, teacher, advisor, or guide of a shaman or of anyone who makes that connection. Amulets may be pieces of bone from a particular animal—they contain the essence of the animal and provide protection or a quality of the animal for the bearer's benefit.

Especially among hunting cultures, people recognize their interdependence with the animals on which they depend, and there will be particular rituals for killing an animal and for treating it respectfully after death. A common theme is an Animal Master in the spiritual realm who watches over the animals, sometimes withholding them from hunters if a taboo has been broken or a ritual missed. A shaman will journey to the Animal Master to make amends.

SEE ALSO: **AMULET; BIRDS**

ANIMISM

ALTHOUGH "ANIMISM" APPEARS often in ethnographies, there is no set definition of the term. It derives from the Latin *anima*, meaning "soul," and is generally understood to mean the attribution of life force and sentience to beings that can influence human events, such as animals, plants, stones, and natural forces such as wind and rain.

AUSTRALIA AND ABORIGINES

SCHOLARS DISAGREE AS to whether Australian Aborigines should be included within even a broad definition of shamanism. Instead, "totemism" is used, meaning "system of belief in which humans are said to have kinship or a mystical relationship with a spirit-being, such as an animal or plant."[4] While ancient rock art in Australia shares characteristics such as X-ray vision with rock art elsewhere, it is attributed to an earlier tradition than that of Australian Aborigines.[5]

Australia is included here, however, because of its direct connection to the land, beautifully expressed as its ancestral Dreamtime or Dreaming. Long ago, Australian ancestors, who possessed special powers and were intimately associated with certain plants and animals, traveled over a featureless land. In doing so, their actions gave it form, creating natural features such as rivers and mountain ranges, thus shaping the land that is occupied today by their descendants.[6]

AXIS MUNDI

THE AXIS MUNDI is the center pole of existence in shamanic and other spiritual traditions. It derives from the Latin *axis*, meaning a straight line or pivot point about which a form rotates, and *mundi*, meaning world. It is also used to mean "center of the world," "cosmic axis," "world axis," and "world pillar." The line passes through the center of the earth, around which the universe revolves, connecting its surface or Middle World with the heavens or Upper World and the underworld or Lower World. It is also the point where the four directions—north, east, south, and west—meet.

It appears to be a universal, although its form will differ cross-culturally from a tree or plant to a pole, ladder, or rope by which shamans ascend to the heavens; they come closer to transcendental union via skills not accessible to an ordinary person and demonstrate their powers of spiritual ascent.

AYAHUASCA

AYAHUASCA, ALSO CALLED *yajé, caapi,* and other local names, is a psychedelic or psychotropic, mind-altering brew native to the Amazon basin. It is made from blending two plants—the shrub *Psychotria viridis* or equivalent depending on the area and the vine *Banisteriopsis caapi* or equivalent. The former contains dimethyltryptamine (DMT), a hallucinogenic tryptamine drug that occurs naturally in many plants and animals. DMT is classified as a Schedule-I drug in the United States; possessing or using it can lead to a fine and up to a year in prison. In Canada, DMT is listed as a Schedule III substance under the Controlled Drugs and Substances Act, and is illegal to possess or trade. In Brazil, however, the ritual use of ayahuasca is legal, and it has become central to organized religious associations.[7] Its use is central to Amazonian shamanism but with many cautions, including this one: While asleep, drunk, or under the effects of psychotropic plants, a person is very vulnerable to supernatural attack; users protect themselves against sorcery with the help of assistants or family members.[8]
SEE ALSO: **SORCERY**

BALANCE, HARMONY

THE SHAMANIC UNIVERSE is a world of opposites such as light/dark, heaven/earth, night/day, male/female, positive/negative, and even good/evil; these must be balanced for the natural order to be maintained.[9] Individuals must be balanced within themselves and in harmony with their family, community, the natural world, and the spirit world; otherwise illness and other troubles result. The natural balance may be upset by disobeying or disregarding cultural protocols, performing improper rituals, or acting disrespectfully toward another sentient being such as a tree or animal.

Nadjeda Duvan is Ulchi, from the Khabarovsk territory of Siberia.[10] She interprets health problems as having "no balance": "You get balance from playing a drum, mouth harp, from different rituals." When things get "out of balance," shamans investigate the causes by journeying to the spirit world to discover what is needed to make restitution. By doing so, the shaman restores the "original" order of the cosmogenesis.

SEE ALSO: **COSMOLOGY AND COSMOGONY**

BILOCATION

BILOCATION, ALSO CALLED dowsing, is the human ability to acquire information about an object's or person's location. Shamans and other practitioners might use this to locate game in a hunting culture or to find a lost object. Pictured on page 9, two Udegai women from the Amur River area of the Russian Far East, Nadezhda Efimovna Kimonko and Valentina Tunsyanovna Kyalundzyuga, describe finding lost objects.[11] (They are not shamans themselves, but grew up with shamans and have ancestors who were shamans.)

Everybody does divination with sticks. We hold them and they move. One time, Dusia lost her money and couldn't remember where she put it. She asked, "Did someone steal it?" and she got the answer "No." "Did I hide it?" she asked. "Yes" was the answer. "On the shelves?" No. "In the mattress?" Yes. She looked and looked and couldn't find it and so she asked again. At last she found it in a little hole in the mattress!"

Valentina (left) and Nadezhda demonstrating their drum, 2008.

BIRDS

BIRDS ARE VERY common motifs on shamans' dresses and their hats or headpieces; feathers or part of a wing or beak may be attached. Some such shamans are called "flying shamans" because they are known to have the ability to fly into the other world. This "magical" flight, as Mircea Eliade describes it, signifies a break between the mundane and the spirit worlds, allowing the shaman to transcend limitations.[12] Birds are symbols of what a shaman aspires to, but they also actualize the shaman's intentions. Eagle and owl are prominent animal spirit helpers, but any bird may become a spirit helper. Rock art shows examples of human/bird merging, and the deer stones show a combined deer/bird ascending to the afterworld.

SEE ALSO: **DEER STONES; ELIADE, MIRCEA; ROCK ART**

BUDDHISM

BUDDHISM, ONE OF the predominant religions of the world, has many variants, some of which contest Buddhism's shamanic roots while others recognize them.

Before 1950 and the Chinese occupation of Tibet, there were two orientations of Buddhism: clerical Buddhism and shamanic Buddhism. Clerical Buddhism, which is also called monastic or scholarly Buddhism, relies on texts. Shamanic Buddhism, on the other hand, involves communication with an alternate reality via alternate states of consciousness in line with Mircea Eliade's universal model of shamanism. The role of a Tibetan lama, Geoffrey Samuel points out, is that of a shaman.[13] The Tibetan Bön tradition notably integrates shamanism with Buddhism.

SEE ALSO: **ELIADE, MIRCEA; TANTRA; TIBETAN BÖN OR BON**

CAMPBELL, JOSEPH (1904–1987)

AN AMERICAN PROFESSOR, Joseph Campbell produced many works on comparative religion and mythology, influencing such disciplines as religious studies, anthropology, and psychology as well as influencing scholars such as Carl Jung, Mircea Eliade, and Michael Harner. One of his essential theories was that all myths and epic stories are connected in the human psyche and manifest the human need to explain metaphysical realities. A shaman, he writes, "may translate some of his visions into ritual performances for his people. That's bringing the inner experience into the outer life of the people themselves."[14]

His 1984 book, *The Way of the Animal Powers: Historical Atlas of World Mythology*, is a cross-cultural study of the spiritual awakening in the earliest of peoples in human evolution, going as far back as the Paleolithic time period. It also documents animist and shamanist cultures that have survived into modern times.

SEE ALSO: **ELIADE, MIRCEA; HARNER, MICHAEL; JUNG, CARL; ROCK ART**

CELTIC

THE CELTS ARE peoples of mainland Europe, Britain, and Ireland whose origins are uncertain and contested, and whose history is constructed through archaeological remains and Irish texts from the eighth century onward. Their cultures were diverse but share a common and recognizable artistic tradition characterized by flowing lines and forms.

Whether the term "shamanism" is applicable to Celtic spirituality is controversial. One author equates what is now called a shaman's role with the role of the Celtic druid,[15] while another source equates the Celtic "quest" with the shamanic journey, using the terms "shaman" and "shamanism" in relation to Celtic traditions because they are commonly used and understood terms today.[16] Others draw parallels between Celtic spirituality and other shamanic traditions, such as that of Native Americans, to construct a Celtic shamanism.[17]

The 19th and 20th centuries in Britain, Ireland, and Europe saw the Celtic Revival, with interest in reviving what was known about Celtic culture as well as expanding on it. A key figure in the revival was Irish writer William Butler Yeats (1865–1939), who was interested in the occult, fairy tales, supernatural Celtic themes, and Irish mythology. Today, the idea of Celtic shamanism figures prominently in neopaganism, neoshamanism, and Wicca.

Cernunnos, the "horned" or "antlered" god, is a classic symbol of what has become known as Celtic shamanism. His earliest-known depictions date to about 400 BCE. Here, he is shown on the Gundestrup Cauldron, found in Denmark and dating to about the first century BCE. Photograph courtesy of Roberto Fortuna and Kira Ursem & the National Museum of Denmark.

CHINA

SHAMANISM IS CHINA'S oldest Indigenous spiritual tradition. While still practiced widely in China today, especially in rural areas and villages, it is primarily associated with the lower classes and looked down upon or even suppressed by the state and local authorities. Chinese shamanism shares the same basic elements with shamanism elsewhere—seeking help from the spirits in trance and via divination, communicating with the ancestors, influencing the weather, and curing illness. In comparison, Confucianism and Taoism are favored by the upper classes; more scholarly attention has been given to the two than to shamanism and other "folk religion" practices. At the same time, both Confucianism and Taoism include shamanist principles and practices. Confucianism, for example, incorporates ancestor worship, which is characteristic of Chinese shamanism. And Taoism incorporates the shamanist principle of duality in the opposing forces—male/female, light/dark, positive/negative—of yin and yang; they are attracted to one another, and each needs the other to define itself. Confucianism, Buddhism, Taoism, and shamanism in China have blended together, with much cross-fertilization from one to the other. Also blended are China's many cultures—as many as 55 "minority nationalities"[18] from Korean to Mongolian in Inner Mongolia to the Hill Tribes, such as the Lisu, Lahu, and Miao, to Tibetan and a small community of Russians among them.

Although its origins are vague, the *I Ching*, known as the *Book of Changes*, has become very popular in the West, with many translations from the original Chinese, including one with a foreword by Carl Jung. It is often touted as the oldest divination system in the world, but its roots are shamanic and derive from earlier methods of divination such as scapulimancy.

SEE ALSO: **DIVINATION; HILL TRIBES OF NORTHERN THAILAND; JUNG, CARL; KOREA; SCAPULIMANCY**

CHRISTIANITY

CHRISTIANITY HAS BEEN and continues to be a proselytizing religion. In its attempts at converting religions, beliefs, or opinions, it has taken many approaches—many brutal and militaristic.

Whereas shamanic traditions view humans and the natural world as inseparable, as "one," Christianity prioritizes the human experience, essentially dividing humans from nature and separating their fates, as in the King James version of the Bible, Genesis 1:26–28:

And God said, let us make man in our image, after our likeness: and let them have dominion over the fish of the sea, and over the fowl of the air, and over the cattle, and over all the earth, and over every creeping thing that creepeth upon the earth ... And God blessed them, and God said unto them, be fruitful, and multiply, and replenish the earth, and subdue it: and have dominion over the fish of the sea, and over the fowl of the air, and over every living thing that moveth upon the earth."

Shamanic and Christian views came into conflict; for example, the tripartite universe of shamanism—the Upper, Middle, and Lower Worlds—became the triad of Heaven, Earth, and Hell and was reinterpreted as the holy trinity of the Father, Son, and Holy Ghost or Holy Spirit. At the same time, there exist many thousands of Christian denominations worldwide with differing attitudes toward shamanism. In the New Testament, for example, Jesus cast out demons—a classic shamanic practice. Early Christian churches in Europe and Britain sought pagan converts by integrating the animist image of the Green Man into the churches. Christianity retained the practice of burning sacred plants as incense, connecting to the unseen world via their sacred smoke as well as through visions and prayer. In the headquarters of the Catholic Church in Rome, the reverend Gabriele Amorth[19] conducted tens of thousands of exorcisms (the shamanic equivalent of extractions) until he died in 2016.[20]

Today, there is an interest in reuniting peoples and cultures that religion has separated. The book *Shamanic Christianity: The Direct Experience of Mystical Communion* by Bradford Keeney is one such attempt at reconciliation and understanding. He suggests that

the shamanic experiences of Christianity can be rekin-
dled to restore direct connection to the spirit world and
shows how shamanic experience is the root of mystical
communion.

SEE ALSO: **GREEN MAN AND GREEN WOMAN; MIDDLE WORLD;
SACRED GEOMETRY; UNDERWORLD OR LOWER WORLD;
UPPER WORLD**

One particularly harrowing account from 1917
describes the persecution of shamans in Southeast Alaska:

A terrible persecutor of shamans in Alaska was the
captain of a military boat stationed in Sitka, Mr. Glass.
Hunting shamans was his favorite pastime and sport.
A captured shaman was usually invited aboard his
boat and received with honor. Glass talked to him in
a friendly manner, inquiring about his life, the number
of his yéik, the extent of their strength and power, etc.
Then he would pronounce that he was also a shaman
who owned yéik and suggested that they compete
against each other. Upon his order, a charged electric
battery was brought out. The shaman was asked to
hold the wires in his hands, while the poles were being
connected. The shaman's body began to twist. His
own people, witnessing his strange and funny poses
and hearing screams and moans, became frightened.
The shaman himself learned a practical lesson about
the power of his white colleague. But the captain did
not stop at that. Shamans often left his boat with their
heads shaved and covered with oil paint, and having
promised not to practice shamanism anymore.

"Of course, such harsh measures discouraged
many shamans but did not totally destroy this occupation in Alaska ... Despite the strenuous efforts of

Christianity to eradicate paganism among the south-eastern Alaskan Indians, some shamans still practice there. One of them from the Killisnoo area is probably still alive, and at least five more can be found in isolated villages."[21]

CIRCLE

The circle is a universal and elemental symbol of unity both in nature and in culture. In shamanism, the circle represents the cyclical nature of existence as in the "circle of life." It is the basis of the Medicine Wheel of First Nations and Native Americans and of the mandala in Eastern religions. In nature, the concentric rings of a tree are in circular form, and the sun and moon are represented as circles in art everywhere. All over the world, Indigenous Peoples base cultural elements on the circle, as in the footprint of a tipi or yurt, the circular drum, or the circle dance.

CIRCUMPOLAR SHAMANISM

The circumpolar world refers to the Arctic regions in Russia (Siberia), the United States (Alaska), Canada, and Greenland.

Siberia is called the "cradle" of this circumpolar complex, out of which people moved eastward and northward up into the Bering Sea area 16,500 years ago and then crossed over into Alaska to continue eastward along the Arctic coasts across Canada and into Greenland. The literature on Arctic peoples is extensive in Russian, English, and Danish, and the archaeological record is rich in artifacts that support the idea of a circumpolar shamanic complex. With their different histories of colonization, however, shamanism has taken on different expressions in each country today.

In Greenland, under Danish rule, evangelical Lutheranism became the official and dominant Christian religion, while a small minority still practice shamanism. In Alaska, the Russian Orthodox Church and the state brutally suppressed shamanism. Edward Curtis (1868–1952) was the lead photographer in an 1899 expedition to Alaska to document what he saw as a disappearing way of life. Among the peoples of the Canadian Arctic, known as "Eskimo" in the ethnographic literature and as "Inuit" today, shamanism was more or less wiped out by the Christian Church and the lineage broken through government policies of assimilation.

The Inuk Aua (also written as Ava and Awa) is called one of the last shamans of the Canadian Inuit.[22] An Inuk of the Igloolik area, Aua practiced into the 1920s when Inuit mythology and its shamanistic beliefs and practices were being taken over by Christianity.

SEE ALSO: **CHRISTIANITY; MONGOLIA; SIBERIA**

Aua had been committed to becoming a shaman but was not accepted by any of the teachers he had approached. Instead he ventured alone into the landscape to find an answer or not return, and suffered the deprivation that characterizes shamanic initiation, whether that initiation is guided by other shamans or by Spirit itself. He relayed his experience of becoming a shaman to Knud Rasmussen (1930):

I endeavored to become a shaman by the help of others, but in this I did not succeed. I visited many famous shamans, and gave them great gifts ... I sought solitude, and here I soon became very melancholy. I would sometimes fall to weeping, and feel unhappy without knowing why. Then, for no reason, all would suddenly be changed, and I felt a great, inexplicable joy, a joy so powerful that I could not restrain it, but had to break into song, a mighty song, with only room for the one word: joy, joy! And I had to use the full strength of my voice. And then in the midst of such a fit of mysterious and overwhelming delight I became a shaman, not knowing myself how it came about … I could see and hear in a totally different way. I had gained my 'quamaneq,' my enlightenment, the shaman-light of brain and body, and this in such a manner that it was not only I who could see through the darkness of life, but the same bright light also shone out from me, imperceptible to human beings but visible to all spirits of earth and sky and sea, and these now came to me and became my helping spirits."

SEE ALSO: **SPIRITS**

Yakut Siberian shaman doll on a wooden base. Anchorage Museum, 1985.

CORE SHAMANISM

"CORE SHAMANISM" IS a term that Michael Harner attributes to Carlos Castaneda,[23] who uses it in his book on Don Juan, the Yaqui sorcerer shaman from Sonora, Mexico.[24] Harner then applies it to practices and principles that are common to shamanic cultures regardless of time or place. Core shamanism includes the shamanic journey, the existence of two realities (Ordinary and Non-Ordinary), and the existence of spirits, including helping spirits.[25] Today, core shamanism has become the main form practiced in most of the West.[26]

Related terms used to describe the fundamentals of shamanism are "prototypical" and "classic." Mircea Eliade uses the former to describe Siberian shamanism,[27] whereas another writer uses "classic" to describe Siberian shamanism.[28] "Pan-shamanism," a term introduced by the author, describes the diversity of shamanic practices and techniques worldwide.

COSMOLOGY AND COSMOGONY

THE ANTHROPOLOGICAL DEFINITION of cosmology refers to a doctrine, theory, account, explanation, model, or system that explains the origin, structure, and nature of the universe or cosmos, its order, and the metaphysical meaning of life. Cosmogony refers to the "coming into being" of the cosmos or universe, but the two terms may be used interchangeably in anthropological literature. (An equivalent lay term is "worldview.") Both terms may include a culture's creation or origin stories, astronomical knowledge, categories of time and space, ideas about the afterlife, and so on. For the purposes of this book, I use the term "shamanist cosmology" to describe commonality of experience, at the same time recognizing that different shamanist cultures may express core ideas differently. The worldview of a hunting culture will differ in some respects from that of farmers or herders, just as Buddhist or Christian cosmologies vary.

Some shamans use maps to navigate the unseen world and may even portray the layout of the afterlife. Paintings by the Peruvian ayahuasca shaman Pablo Amaringo are particularly detailed portrayals of the three worlds and the beings that inhabit them.[29]

SEE ALSO: **AYAHUASCA**

CRYSTALS

THE INTERNAL STRUCTURE of crystals is the most mathematically pure and regular of any solid form, while they are notably beautiful in their outside appearance. Crystals, especially quartz crystals, are valuable to science for their unique properties and their industrial and technological applications. They are also revered as power objects in many cultures worldwide.[30] Perhaps crystals reveal their properties to the seeker in the same way that shamanist traditions receive teachings directly from plants.

Crystals may be used for "seeing" into the past, present, or future. They may be laid on the body as a healing tool, be carried on the body for protection or worn as an amulet, or form part of a shaman's tool kit. In Mongolia, the Darhad shaman Maamaa has collected a large bag of quartz crystals from his ancestral lands to be used in shamanizing, and when his children are sick, he has them walk barefoot on white sand to remove the illness.

Among the Aranda of Australia, initiation for those being transformed into medicine men or shamans included the introduction of magic crystals into their bodies by other medicine men or by Dream Time spirits.[31] Flying by virtue of a quartz crystal is a common shamanic technique in Australia that is also found elsewhere.[32]

Archaeologists report that crystals are frequently found at sites of special significance to ancient peoples, with quartz occurring frequently at Neolithic and Bronze Age monuments in Britain and Ireland.[33]

SEE ALSO: **AUSTRALIA AND ABORIGINES**

CULTURAL APPROPRIATION

CULTURAL APPROPRIATION, SOMETIMES termed "cultural misappropriation," is the inappropriate, un-acknowledged exploitation of another culture's practices, ideas, dress, music, art or artifacts, rituals, and so on, without proper respect and acknowledgment and without regard for the original purpose, context, or meaning. Usually appropriation is by a dominant group of a disadvantaged, minority, or marginalized group, frequently within a colonialist context. Like other terms discussed in this book, "cultural appropriation" is not a definitive term; it is also controversial in the literature but should be understood and respected, especially as it relates to shamanism.

DANCE, MOVEMENT

DANCE MOVEMENTS MAY be spontaneous and freeform or ritualized and synchronized. Dance may be for entertainment, or it may have a sacred purpose such as relating a group's history through movement or enacting an important cultural event.

Tibetan sacred dance is one of the most formalized dance traditions, combining the shamanic Bön tradition with Buddhism. *Cham*, or "lama" dance, is the sacred monastic dance performed by Tibetan monks. One of its most important and beautiful dances reenacts the conflict for power by the earlier Tibetan Bön shamanist tradition and later Buddhism. It illustrates the idea that killing another human being for the sake of others dispels greater evil and saves thousands of lives,[34] in contrast to the Buddhist tenet to not take life.

Cham dances are prescribed in every detail. Foot, hand, and body movements represent qualities of deities (male and female), while dancers must lift up their costumes from the right side and then switch, putting on their clothes over their heads from the left side. Masks are not inanimate but embody the deity they represent, while colors of the costumes have particular meanings—blue, for example, represents limitless space. As in other shamanic traditions, images of animals act as guardians, in this case, of the mandala.[35]

In contrast, the circle dance in which I took part outside Moscow, Russia, in 2000 brought together representatives of many of the Indigenous Peoples of Siberia; it included foreigners such as myself as well as Russian organizers. The call-and-response format allowed everyone to participate regardless of their language, while leadership of the chant and the dance emerged spontaneously from within the group.

SEE ALSO: **MANDALAS; TIBETAN BÖN OR BON**

Tibetan Bön dancer, Menri Monastery, northern India, 2005.

DEATH AND DYING

SHAMANS MUST DIE to their old selves in order to be born in a new form—that of the shaman. By dying to the physical world, a shaman is born into the world of spirit and vice versa, a newborn emerges from the spirit world into this physical world). This can mean undergoing extreme hardships and facing difficult challenges that can be overcome only through help from the spirit world.

Death might be literal or symbolic, but either way, it is "real." Through the experience, the shaman loses the fear of death, becomes familiar with the afterlife, and can accompany others or prepare the way for them to make the safe transition. This is known as psychopomp work.
SEE ALSO: **INITIATION; PSYCHOPOMP**

Knud Rasmussen describes how two Padlermiut of the Canadian Arctic died in the process of becoming shamans:

 Kinalik had once dreamed about a man in the tribe, dreamed that he would become ill. This was taken as a sign of her disposition for shamanism, the dream having been put into her by spirits. The shaman Igju-garjuk, her brother-in-law, therefore made up his mind to make her a shaman. The people of the village were called together, and Kinalik's old mother Abggarjuk then asked Igjugarjuk to shoot her. She had previously spent five whole days out, suspended in tent poles, raised above the ground, in order that Hila might see her and take notice of her. It was winter, cold blizzards were blowing, but she noticed nothing of the cold because her helping spirits were with her.

"When she was to be shot, she was placed on a skin, sitting by iga, the separate kitchen that is built into the entrance passage; she was placed between iga and the living room itself. She had not to be shot with a lead bullet, but with something from the earth, a little stone. Igjugarjuk therefore shot her with a small round stone in the presence of all the villagers, and she fell over, dead. After that there was a song-feast. Kinalik lay dead the whole night. She suffered nothing, her future helping spirits protected her. The next morning, just when Igjugarjuk was about to call her to life again, she woke up of her own accord. It now appeared that she had been shot in the heart. Later the stone was taken out and is now preserved by her old mother.

"Through this death Kinalik had become acceptable to helping spirits; Hila had noticed her, and the helping spirits might come to her of themselves. Her principal helping spirit was her dead brother ... She spoke freely and cheerfully about how her dead brother used to come to her, for among the Caribou Eskimos [*sic*] they are not afraid to mention the dead by name. He used to come to her gliding through the air, legs uppermost, head downwards, but as soon as he had reached the ground he could walk like an ordinary man. Her other helping spirit was the polar bear ...

"Igjugarjuk did not carry her training further, as he thought it a pity to let her suffer more. For of course the fact is that the more one suffers for one's art, the greater shaman one becomes.

"Igjugarjuk has also trained Aggiartoq, a young man, to be a shaman. In this case he used the third form of suffering, viz. drowning. Aggiartoq was tied fast to a long tent pole and then carried by Igjugarjuk and Ulibvaq—an elderly man in the village—down to a big lake. There a hole was hewn in the ice and, clad in caribou-skin frock, mittens and full outfit, Aggiartoq, bound to the tent pole, was pushed down through the hole so that he stood on the bottom of the lake. There they let him stay five whole days, and when they took him up again he was as dry as if he had never been in water. This young man's helping spirits were the spirit of his dead mother and a human skeleton."[36]

DEER

IN MANY TRADITIONS, the deer is a sacred animal that is capable of bridging Ordinary Reality and Non-Ordinary Reality, perhaps because it appears so silently to a hunter and then as quickly leaps away to disappear into the distance. The Celtic "horned god" or "animal master," called Cernunnos, is part human in form with deer antlers at the head and is surrounded by animals such as a snake and another antlered deer. The dancer of the sacred Deer Dance of Tibet wears a head-dress in the form of a deer from which antlers extend upward toward the Sky World; here, the deer is a protective deity. In the yarn paintings of the Huichol of Mexico, antlered human figures and deer are common motifs with deer considered as the most sacred beings in the animal world and closely associated with the divine peyote cactus.[37] The deer stones of Mongolia, dating back more than 3,000 years, portray flying or ascending deer with their antlers connecting to the Upper Worlds.

SEE ALSO: **BUDDHISM; DEER STONES**

DEER STONES

THE ROOTS OF shamanism run deep in Central Asia. Archaeological, linguistic, genetic, and ethnographic evidence pinpoints this part of the world as the birthplace of a circumpolar shamanic complex that extends into northern Russia across the Old Bering Sea area into the North American Arctic and moving south from there into the Americas. The "deer stones," which extend across the steppes as far as eastern Europe and Germany, date back to the Bronze Age, when nomads erected hundreds of them, possibly to commemorate the lives of individuals, among them perhaps shamans, or to assist the deceased in making the journey to the other world.

Some of the finest deer stones are found in central and northern Mongolia.

The iconic imagery of the stones includes flying deer with birdlike characteristics that may symbolize shamanic transcendence. They may be showing the spirit of someone, perhaps a shaman, moving through the three planes of existence. The discs, which appear on most stones, possibly represent shamans' mirrors while shield-like ornaments such as stylized daggers may have given protection in the afterlife or on the deceased's journey to the spirit world. The deer stones may have acted as portals into the unseen world of the ancestors and other spirits, or served as a focal point of shamanic ritual.[38]

SEE ALSO: **MIRROR**

Called "deer stones" by archaeologist William Fitzhugh of the Smithsonian Arctic Studies Center, these stone megaliths were erected by Bronze Age nomads in the northern area of Mongolia and southern Siberia in about 1000 BCE.[39] This photo was taken in 2006.

DISMEMBERMENT

DISMEMBERMENT IS A classic shamanic technique by which a shaman-in-the-making has their body taken apart in the spirit world; it may even be hacked to pieces. The initiate is then reconstituted as a new person—a shaman with the gift of healing.

DIVERSITY OF SHAMANIC TRADITIONS

BECAUSE "SHAMANISM" IS an umbrella term created by Western anthropologists as a classification tool, shamanism is so diverse historically and geographically it is difficult to make generalizations while respecting cultural protocols and individual differences among shamans even within the same culture. At the same time, core principles and practices transcend time and space. Historical factors such as religious persecution, assimilation policies, and conflict with the dominant culture or state, as well as environmental differences, all contribute to variations on a culture's relationship to the spirit world.
SEE ALSO: **CORE SHAMANISM**

DIVINATION

DIVINATION IS WIDESPREAD geographically and historically, and employs a variety of techniques to see into the past, present, or future with the intent of altering the fate of a patient. Divination is not fortune-telling; instead, it is "soothsaying"—that is, revealing the truth. Divination may "read" the hidden meaning of objects such as bones (scapulimancy is a particular type of divination), stones, the placement of twigs as they are dropped from the hand, or the movements of animals to predict the future and provide answers to questions such as how to find a lost object, the best place to go for success in hunting, or how to solve a personal problem. Answers may come in a dream, from a shaman's vision quest, or during a shaman's journey. A shaman may use clairvoyance (seeing or perceiving things or future events outside of the usual ways of sensory contact) or predict the outcome of an event to guide a person's actions.

Joseph Campbell describes divination by an Altaic shaman that illustrates the connections among divination, soul loss, illness and healing, the sucking technique of curing, projection, drumming, journeying, and soul retrieval. It shows classic shamanist techniques while placing them in a particular tradition. Altai is now a Russian republic in southern Siberia ("he" should be read as neutral of gender):

When an Altaic shaman has been summoned to a sickbed, his first task is to determine by divination the cause of the illness. If he finds that an object of some sort has been projected into the patient's body by the magic of another shaman, the healer will first perform a series of rites, to the beating of his drum, to break the power of the magic, and then will apply his lips to the affected part and suck until—eureka!—he will spit from his mouth some pebble or even worm or roach that will represent the affliction. If it is found, however, that the reason for the indisposition is that the patient's soul has been abducted by the Messengers either of Ülgen above or of Ärlik below, the shaman will have to undertake a visionary voyage in trance to retrieve it."[40]

Neoshamans employ dowsing, pendulums, and crystal balls, all derived from archaic divination techniques. Divination may be enhanced by assuming the correct posture while in trance; effective divining postures include half-kneeling or sitting on a stool.[41]

SEE ALSO: **SCAPULIMANCY**

DREAMS

SCIENCE HAS NOT unanimously identified the purpose of dreams, although there are many theories about why we dream. Shamanic cultures see dreams as portals into the spirit world. A shaman may receive a spirit helper or a song in a dream, be told what medicine to make to cure an illness, receive messages from the ancestors about how to manage a difficult situation, or the dream may portend events to come. Such dreams may happen spontaneously or be requested, while in lucid dreaming, dreamers are aware that they are dreaming. Sometimes "dream" and "vision" are used interchangeably.

DRUM

Johnny Lagaxnitz singing with a drum. Kitwanga, c. 1924.
Image courtesy of Canadian Museum of History.

ARCHAEOLOGY HAS NO record of the very first drums because the natural materials of which early drums would have been made don't last. Instead, we find evidence of figures holding what appear to be drums in archaic rock art in many parts of the world. Drumming is a universal, used in healing, transformation, relaxation, celebration, and shamanic journeying; however, the styles of drums and how they are played vary widely from the horizontal hollowed-out log drums[42] of the Amur region in Siberia, played only by women, to the mother drums of North America, which are played by as many as 12 people at a time, to the bronze temple drums of Southeast Asia.

A Siberian shaman explained how "the drum is my ride," meaning the drum is the horse that carries the shaman into an altered state while the drumbeater urges it on. The rhythm of the drum echoes the sound of horses' hooves galloping across the grasslands.

Scientific research has measured the drum tempo required to induce an altered state of consciousness. A steady beat of 4.5 Hertz or beats per second for at least 15 minutes facilitates an altered state of consciousness into theta brainwave activity, which has been likened to a trance state of reverie. Shamanic drumming has specific neurophysiological effects and can elicit temporary changes in brain-wave activity.[43] Drumming may also elicit subjective experiences and images with common themes, including loss of time continuum; movement sensations such as pressure on or expansion of various parts of the body and body image distortion; sensations of flying, spiraling, dancing, running, and so on; feelings of being energized, relaxed, sharp and clear, hot, cold, or in physical, mental, and/or emotional discomfort; emotions ranging from reverie to rage; and vivid images of animals, people, and landscapes.[44]

While participants in a shamanic ritual view the front side of the drum, the back of the drum facing the shaman

The Drummer—Nunivak, Alaska. Edward Curtis, 1929.

Siberian shamans' drums showing the front and back sides, 2003.

identifies the shaman and describes how the drum and shaman unite to contact, please, appease, and entreat the spirits.

SEE ALSO: **RATTLES**

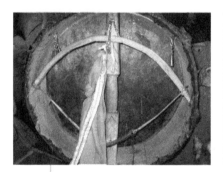

On this back of a drum belonging to a woman shaman from the Darhad Valley, Mongolia, the central column is an arrow, and the curved wooden crosspiece is the bow, which shoots the shaman into the spirit world, where the shaman hunts for guidance and assistance. The chevron pattern on the central spine is the horse's mane.

Back of a Siberian shaman's drum, 2003.

ECSTASY

ECSTASY, OR THE ecstatic state, is a term used extensively in the ethnographic literature to describe the altered state of consciousness (ASC) achieved by shamans. The state is also called the Shamanic State of Consciousness (SSC).

EFFIGY

AN EFFIGY IS a representation of a specific individual in the form of a sculpture or figurine, perhaps a doll or other miniature. In shamanism, an effigy may portray a god or ancestral spirit. Small figures are sometimes called "spirit dolls" in the literature but were generally not intended for use by children; instead, they were "medicine" used by shamans and other healers.

"Spirit doll" made for the author by Emile Gautreau, Métis medicine man, Nova Scotia, Canada. This one was used like the worry dolls of Guatemala: You would ask it to take your problems from you and place them in a tree or elsewhere in nature for the problems to be carried away by the winds or rain.

ELIADE, MIRCEA (1907–1986)

MIRCEA ELIADE WAS a philosopher and professor who published extensively on the history of religions and on comparative religion. His pioneering work in shamanism has influenced many scholars from Carl Jung to Joseph Campbell to Michael Harner and Sandra Ingerman. His models of shamanism are still in use today; however, his work is controversial because he worked in the abstract rather than from direct experience.

In his books *Shamanism: Archaic Techniques of Ecstasy* and *Rites and Symbols of Initiation: The Mysteries of Birth and Rebirth*, Eliade uses the term "primitive" to refer to archaic, Indigenous, animist, and shamanic cultures and practices, and he makes comparisons between shamanism and what he calls the "higher religions" of India, European Christianity, and ancient Greece—both terms are unacceptable today.

EXTRACTION, EXORCISM

EXTRACTION IS A classic shamanic technique whereby a shaman removes an extra-pernicious influence (epi), bad energy, negative influence, unwanted influence, entity, or evil spirit, sometimes called a devil or demon, from the body of a person. Such spirits may be malevolent, or they may just be lost souls who never crossed to the afterlife properly and have taken refuge in the patient, who lacked the power to ward them off. Shamans conducting extractions must be power-filled themselves; if not, such things may transfer from patient to shaman. Exorcism is a Christian practice, primarily of the Catholic Church, which authorizes exorcism for parishioners believed to be demonically possessed.

THE EYE CURTAIN or eye covering worn by shamans when journeying removes them from Ordinary Reality. Some will have a fringe made of strips of hide or ribbon or from strings of beads. It may be more symbolic rather than functional so as not to interfere with the shaman's vision.

Most Siberian shamans use the fringe to protect the onlookers, for when a spirit enters the shaman, people should not look at the shaman's eyes or face; because of the spirit's power, they would be frightened or harmed.[45] The fringe or dangles of the eye curtain facilitate an altered state of consciousness by breaking up Ordinary Reality—allowing shamans to see enough of Ordinary Reality to know where they are but not preventing or overtaking the experience of Non-Ordinary Reality.[46]

As the shaman dances or shakes in trance, the fringe moves rhythmically, producing a sort of strobe-light effect for the shaman behind the eye curtain and also adding to the multisensory experience of the participants.

The Dukha Shaman, Haltsan, of northern Mongolia, in his shaman's dress showing the eye curtain. The eyes on the face mask allow the shaman to see into Non-Ordinary Reality, 2007.

FETISH

ANTHROPOLOGICAL AND LAY definitions of "fetish" differ, and it has had different meanings throughout history. Once applied by Europeans to objects used to make and reinforce agreements in West Africa, "fetish" was used in a condescending manner to imply that Africans were unable to grasp complex ideas about religion and "art." Later, curators of African art acknowledged their religious and aesthetic sophistication.[47]

Today, the term may be used interchangeably with "talisman," "charm," or "amulet." Specifically, a fetish is an inanimate object valued for its magical powers or because it is inhabited by a spirit.

This tiny bear made by Emery Eriacho was purchased by the author in 2007 in New Mexico, where the turquoise stone is mined. It measures only 1 inch in length.

The Zuni are Native Americans who inhabit lands in New Mexico. They carve local stone such as turquoise into a variety of fetish animals; the spirits of these animals assist the owners on their hunt, offering protection and healing. Primary fetish representations are eagle, bear, wolf, mountain lion, badger, and mole, but others may be included, even some that are not native to Zuni lands. Small bundles on the backs of fetishes represent their spiritual power and usually contain a tiny arrowhead with a hunting association, as does this one. While an Indigenous practice, today fetish carving is commercially successful for the Zuni; however, only fetishes that have not been ceremonially blessed may be sold.

FIRE

IN MANY SHAMANIC traditions, fire is a living, powerful being that can be both harmful and beneficial to humans. Feeding the fire is a classic shamanic ritual, sometimes conducted by the shaman and at other times by a shaman's helper. Sacred herbs tossed into the fire produce the smoke on which a shaman travels to the other world. A skin drum may be held over the fire to cleanse and purify it and also to tighten it to produce a better resonance. Mircea Eliade writes that "access to sacrality is manifested, among other things, by a prodigious increase in heat," which can be interpreted as life force or power. He also notes that shamans are considered to be "masters over fire."[48]

GENDER

IN THE ETHNOGRAPHIC and lay literature, the English pronoun "he" is often used indiscriminately to refer to male and female shamans, as well as shamans who do not fit into a gender binary, often called "third gender." This has created many misconceptions about shamanism. In fact, many traditions say that women were the "first" shamans and are the most powerful. Occasionally, one will read the term "shamaness" or "woman shaman," but generally "shaman" is gender neutral. Different cultures vary on the kinds of curings a male or female shaman may conduct, which ceremonies a man or woman may participate in, or whether shamans occupy a third gender.

Hupa shaman. The photo of this Athapascan Hupa woman shaman from northwestern California was taken by photographer Edward Curtis and dates to approximately 1923.

Shaman Tatiana Kobezhikova conducting a ceremony in front of the "gate" to Salbyk Valley, Republic of Khakassia, in 2001 as part of "Ecology and Traditional Religious and Magical Knowledge," a symposium organized by the Russian Academy of Sciences.

GREEN MAN AND GREEN WOMAN

THE ARCHETYPAL IMAGE of the Green Man is found in many cultures and in many time periods from Britain to Tibet, Nepal and India, the Mediterranean, and Mexico, although the form varies. It predates the Christian era but was incorporated into many early Christian churches and cathedrals, perhaps to entice the pagans to whom the image was familiar. Today the image is found in British universities, London pubs, and even banks in Halifax, Canada, among many other surprising places.

A Kwakiutl Hamatsa shaman, also called "Woodman," is shown emerging from the woods after months of seclusion, fasting, and training.[49] He wears a transformation mask "for which the Kwakiutl are renowned"[50] and must be a Northwest Coast representation of the Green Man. Photograph by Edward S. Curtis.

An archetype, Green Man represents renewal and rebirth and the eternal circle of life. In his oldest forms, he is a face formed of leaves. In later forms, he emerges from foliage, often oak or ivy, sometimes disgorging it from his mouth, eyes, and ears. Either way he is a composite image of man and nature. The figures are predominantly male, although some are of a (rarer) Green Woman. Perhaps the genders are united in that the archetypal male emerges from the archetypal feminine, natural world.

One of more than 100 Green Man images found in the 15th-century Rosslyn Chapel, Edinburgh, Scotland, 2002.

HALLUCINOGENS

HALLUCINOGENS ARE DRUGS that cause hallucinations or alter moods and perception, such as d-lysergic acid diethylamide (LSD), psilocybin, peyote, or datura. Some shamanic traditions and some practitioners of neo-shamanism use hallucinogens to induce an altered state of consciousness; others rely on techniques such as drumming, chanting, or sensory deprivation.

HARNER, MICHAEL (1929–2018)

MICHAEL HARNER WAS an anthropologist. His book, *The way of the Shaman*, first published in 1980, is a classic in shamanic studies. It launched the modern shamanic renaissance, introducing shamanism to a Western audience and changing the West's ideas about reality.

The book views shamanism not as a religion but as a methodology. Shamanic techniques can enhance contemporary holistic health practices to help with stress reduction, anxiety, and depression by accessing assistance from non-ordinary sources and by altering consciousness so that we reconsider what is real.

Harner's early firsthand experiences with shamanism were primarily in North and South America, but as he was the founder of the Foundation for Shamanic Studies, his contribution became worldwide. The foundation is dedicated to the preservation, study, and teaching of shamanic knowledge for the welfare of the planet and its inhabitants.

HILL TRIBES OF NORTHERN THAILAND

THE HILL TRIBES, or "highlanders," are ethnic minorities in and migrants to northern Thailand from China. The Hmong, Akha, Karen, Lahu, Lisu, and Mien are the major groups. They are shamanist by tradition with many now practicing Buddhism or Christianity along with shamanism or sometimes in place of it.

They are primarily subsistence farmers whose shamanism differs from that of hunting cultures with core elements remaining. Plant knowledge is of particular importance: More than 1,000 plant species have been identified as in use by the six largest Hill Tribes,[51] and plants play a significant role in encounters with the spirit world. Akha villages, for example, always have a nearby sacred tree that is protected by a fence. A shaman makes offerings to the spirits at an altar within the enclosure. The Karen place a piece of the introduced Century Plant (*Agave americana*) over the doorway of anyone who is being bothered by evil spirits.[52] (In the same way, the Tlingit of Southeast Alaska place a piece of Devil's Club [*Oplopanax horridus*] over a doorway for protection and to prevent bad spirits from entering the household.)

SEE ALSO: **NORTHWEST COAST CULTURE AREA; NUMBERS**

HORSE

IN SIBERIA AND Mongolia, the horse is a sacred animal. Genghis Khan (who died in 1227) unified disparate peoples to create the largest contiguous land-based empire the world has ever known. Mongolians attribute his success to the advice of a shaman or to him being one himself. Shamans here call their drum their "ride" into the other world—drumbeats simulate the sounds of horses' hooves galloping across the steppes while the drumbeater urges the horse to go faster in transporting the rider into an altered state of consciousness. In Siberia, after a shamanic ceremony, fermented mare's milk is shared among the participants as a ritual of unity and to celebrate the presence of Spirit.

In the Lascaux cave paintings in France, which date to Paleolithic times, the horse is one of the most common animals.

SEE ALSO: **MONGOLIA**

ILLNESS, SHAMANIC

IN MANY TRADITIONS, someone may be identified as a potential shaman because of a serious condition or life-threatening illness. When the person recovers, it is with spirit help, and they then take on the role of the shaman. Someone who has suffered will have compassion and the assistance of spirits to help others. Many shamans say that if they did not take on the role, they would become ill again. Recovery from such an illness may require dismemberment and other initiations.

SEE ALSO: **DISMEMBERMENT; INITIATION**

INDIA

INDIA IS KNOWN for its diversity of religions, including Hinduism (which is dominant), Islam, Christianity, Sikhism, Buddhism, Jainism, and Zoroastrianism, according to census data. Shamanism and animism are not indicated on the census, though perhaps they are included under Other.

Shamanism in India is controversial. One view suggests that orthodox Hinduism, as the dominant religion of the majority, has never supported shamanism, "terming it *kshudra-shakti*, literally, low grade power (seeking)." Hindus practice penance, meditation, or devotion to positive entities or gods to acquire positive energies or power, while shamanists appease low-level deities (*yakshas*, for example) to obtain supernatural powers.[53]

Shamanism is still practiced in India, if not very openly, while the major religions retain shamanistic elements, as do the still-practiced folk or Indigenous religions. Indigenous Peoples, who account for a small percentage of India's population, may be considered as animist, as Aboriginal, or as practitioners of Indigenous religions, but these are often syncretized with one of the major religions. In Goa, I visited a male village shaman in 2011 and was told that the villagers go to him when they have some problems. They will also go to a Hindu temple or Christian church.

Neoshamanism, associated with the West, has established a presence in India today.

SEE ALSO: **NEOSHAMANISM AND NEOSHAMANS**

Poh, a shaman in India, performing a ritual to heal a sick child. Alice S. Kandell, 1971.

This "spirit doll" is from the Konkan coastal area of western India. People hang it at the doorway so when someone enters the house, this little figure takes any bad spirits so they won't be carried inside. The little face on the tummy is similar to faces placed on buildings in Goa to scare away bad spirits. I was told that it is a kind of demon, wearing a skeleton/skulls around its neck. In size, it is about three inches tall, 2011.

INDIGENOUS PEOPLES

THE TERM "INDIGENOUS" refers to the original inhabitants of a place with distinct political, social, and economic systems and distinct histories from colonial settler societies. They often have strong links to natural resources and settings. The use of the term is problematic because many of the world's 370 million Indigenous Peoples have been displaced from their homelands through war, appropriation of their lands, colonization, or genocide.

The United Nations Declaration on the Rights of Indigenous Peoples (UNDRIP), adopted in 2007, is now the most comprehensive international instrument on the rights of Indigenous Peoples. It is a universal framework of minimum standards for the survival, dignity, and well-being of the world's Indigenous Peoples, addressing their unique cultures and relations with the environment. Nevertheless, they continue to face marginalization, exclusion, and challenges to their rights to self-determination and autonomy.[54]

At the same time, in many places, the cultures of Indigenous Peoples are undergoing a revitalization. Some continue to practice shamanism, and some families or communities have shamans to advocate for their well-being. In other contexts, people no longer use the term, which may have been replaced by terms such as "medicine man" or "medicine woman" with some practices remaining. For many, if not most, Indigenous groups, their spirituality has blended with the dominant religions and dominant cultures.

AUTHOR OF 12 books, including *Soul Retrieval: Mending the Fragmented Self* (published first in 1991), Sandra Ingerman has pioneered the integration of cross-cultural healing methods with Western psychological concepts and into contemporary therapies and counseling. She addresses soul damage and soul loss as an underlying cause of depression, dissociation, memory repression, addictions, and other traumas, employing the classic shamanic healing technique of soul retrieval in treatment.
SEE ALSO: **SOUL LOSS AND SOUL RETRIEVAL**

INITIATION

INITIATION OF A shaman is a universal, although it will differ in details. Mircea Eliade discusses three types of initiation by spontaneous vocation; that is, by being "called," by hereditary transmission, and through a personal quest. Initiation must involve two aspects of instruction—the ecstatic experience through dreams, trances, or visions—and the group's lexicon of shamanic techniques, spirits, secret language, and genealogy.[55]

The first of the three types is the most common in modern times. Because of the persecution of shamans, ancestral shamanic lineages have been broken in many parts of the world. In researching the peoples of northern Siberia, Juha Pentikäinen, for example, could interview only two contemporary shamans—one Khanty and the other Nanay—as they were the only two to survive the extreme persecution of the 1930s in Siberia by Stalin,[56] a time in Russia when many, many shamans were murdered or sent to the infamous gulag because their power was seen as a threat to the authority of the centralized state. Today, in Siberia, shamans are initiating non-descendants in order to pass on the lineage and reestablish the tradition.

A shamanic initiation in Siberia, 2008.

Dreams, trances, and visions are induced through a variety of ways including via vision quests whereby initiates go into seclusion to meet their spirits. Cleansing and purification are required and may include fasting or dehydration for an extended period of time, immersion in cold water, sensory deprivation in darkness, or the use of psychedelics.

One characteristic aspect of initiation is the initiate's symbolic reduction to the state of a skeleton,[57] whereby an initiate is stripped of all flesh and reduced to their essence to be reformed as a shaman.

SEE ALSO: **PSYCHEDELIC SHAMANISM; SKELETAL MOTIF; X-RAY VISION**

INNER SHAMAN

STANLEY KRIPPNER DEFINES shamans as "those socially designated practitioners who obtain information from their dreams and visions, sharing this knowledge with members of their community." Within this definition, which is more limited than broader definitions used by Joseph Campbell, Michael Harner, Mircea Eliade, and others, Krippner considers that anyone who dreams partakes in shamanism.[58] His term "inner shaman" is defined by José Luis Stevens as "the part of you that connects directly to the true source of the universe."[59] In this sense, shamanism has developed within the neoshamanism movement. It draws on traditional shamanism, but the focus is more on the individual and on shamanism as a guide to personal transformation. In traditional shamanism, the shaman takes on primary responsibility for the well-being of the collective.

INTELLECTUAL PROPERTY RIGHTS (IPR)

INTELLECTUAL PROPERTY RIGHTS (IPR) refers to the rights of a culture, especially minority and marginalized cultures, to determine who may know, make use of, distribute, and represent their collective knowledge and experience, its products and applications, and for what purpose. It especially applies to Indigenous Peoples since elements of their cultures have been appropriated by dominant cultures worldwide without permission, attribution, or compensation. IPR may include songs and stories, emblems, traditional plant knowledge, objects, language, rituals and ceremonies, beliefs, ideas, naming of places, and so on but also encompass ways of being in the world.

INTRUSIONS

INTRUSIONS ARE ALSO called unwanted influences, extra-pernicious influences (epis), bad spirits, evil spirits or entities, devils and demons, and equivalent terms depending on the cultural context. They may be sent by a sorcerer, or an individual might experience soul loss and so be susceptible to harmful thoughts or actions. Such entities lodge in the body and may cause physical or spiritual troubles such as illness, depression, suicidal thoughts, and other negative feelings or actions. They take over a person's power, although a person suffering from an unwanted influence may not be consciously aware of it. Shamans use a variety of techniques to remove intrusions, which may include fighting with them, persuasion, or removal by force. Sucking tubes are often used for this purpose.

SEE ALSO: **SOUL LOSS AND SOUL RETRIEVAL; SUCKING TUBE; SOUL CATCHER**

ISLAM

THIERRY ZARCONE AND Angela Hobart's book *Shamanism and Islam* refers to the assimilation of shamanistic beliefs and rituals into folk Islam as a form of religious syncretism, focusing on the Turkic-speaking peoples of Central Asia, Siberia, and the Middle East. Folk Islam is taken to mean the traditional or mystical form of Islam practiced by local, smaller-scale, rural communities and the urban poor in contrast to the established orthodoxy of Islam.

It emphasizes an inner search and a direct connection to Allah, incorporating classic beliefs and practices of shamanism, including animism, amulets, and ecstatic rituals. A Sufi folk preacher[60] practiced exorcisms (called "extractions" in shamanist terminology): "Bawa would trap the evil spirits in jars as they departed the skulls of patients. He would then seal and bury them in the sands of the nearby beach."[61]

Under the umbrella of folk Islam, some scholars include Sufism, generally defined as the mystical dimension of Islam. As a spiritual offering and meditation, the Sufi "whirling dervish" dances are a form of ecstatic dance and perhaps the best-known form of Sufism to outsiders.

As with all established religions, equation with shamanism is highly contested; at the same time, it is becoming a more common field of academic study.

SEE ALSO: **DANCE, MOVEMENT; EXTRACTION, EXORCISM; SYNCRETISM**

JOURNEY, SHAMANIC

WHAT HAPPENS ON a shamanic journey? In an altered state of consciousness and outside time and space, a shaman travels to the spirit world in search of knowledge to assist with the problems of this world, often in response to a specific question or request for help. As such, a shamanic journey is intentional. The knowledge brought back may be an instruction to do something, a path to be followed, an insight, or a reason for an occurrence. It may be in the form of a song, an object, or a description of an event. Often it is metaphoric; such information is then "translated" by the shaman or inquirer into explanation and action. In the mythological sense, a shamanic journey is a quest and is generally accepted to be the defining characteristic of shamanism.

Shamans may use maps to navigate the spirit world. The Huichol of western Mexico create yarn paintings of their visionary journeys. One such inspired work portrays the journey to bring back the soul of an ancestral shaman, in the form of a rock crystal, who wished to return to earth.[62]

The map that the Tsaatan shaman Haltsan uses to navigate the other world marks good pasture for the reindeer on which the Tsaatan depend. Drums of the Sami, or Lapps, of northern Europe and part of Russia lay out the three levels of the universe; their interconnectedness is portrayed with holes to show entry points by which the shaman travels from level to level. Paintings by the ayahuasca shaman Pablo Amaringo are his visions of detailed layouts of the spirit worlds and the beings that reside there.[63] Or shamans may use mind maps whereby one's helpers and places of significance are laid out on the "inner" landscape.

Portals or entries into the other world, and where a shaman begins his journey, might be a tree's roots, a cave or hole in the ground, a crack between the rocks, or an animal's underground hideout. They may climb a ladder, tree, or rope to make the transition to celestial heights.

As shamans make preparations to enter the other world, they must also be prepared to return safely from a shamanic journey. Those who lack the proper preparation, skills, experience, or guidance, shamans say, can get lost in the other world. They may become psychotic or otherwise disconnected from Ordinary Reality, having left their soul or a part of it in the other world. Shamans use different ways to ensure a safe return; for example, by always following the same route or by using a spoken phrase that means "I have returned" and by relying on their spirit helpers.

SEE ALSO: **ELIADE, MIRCEA; TREE; TSAATAN REINDEER HERDERS**

JUDAISM AND SHAMANISM

AS WITH OTHER major religions that are exploring their roots in shamanism, so is Judaism considering its shamanic ancestry, although to a lesser degree. Orthodox rabbi Gershon Winkler studied with Native American healers of the Southwest; from them he started to recover what he calls "Aboriginal Judaism," which he describes as Judaism's roots.[64] Celia Rothenberg discusses "Jewish shamanism" in relation to what she calls "New Age Jews."[65]

JUNG, CARL (1875–1961)

CARL JUNG WAS a Swiss psychoanalyst and psychotherapist whose work informed many fields of study, including anthropology. His last work, *Man and His Symbols*, completed just before he died, examines the unconscious and how symbols revealed in dreams carry practical advice from the unconscious to the conscious level. The book itself resulted from one of Jung's own dreams. It also addresses symbols that appear throughout history and includes a section on shamanism.

Jung made traditional and archaic shamanic practices understood and valued in modern psychiatry and psychotherapy. The shaman, he writes, "is not only a familiar denizen [occupant of a particular place] but even the favored scion of those realms of power that are invisible to our normal waking consciousness, which all may visit briefly in vision, but through which he roams, a master."[66]

SEE ALSO: **DREAMS**

KOREA

KOREAN SHAMANISM HAS received a great deal of attention in the scholarly literature. Today in South Korea, shamanism is recognized as a vital and relevant practice. (North Korea/DPRK discourages the practice of shamanism.) Buddhism is popular in South Korea, and the two have blended, with shamanist elements incorporated into Buddhist architecture and art. Korean shamanism incorporates geomancy, whereby buildings such as graves, temples, and dwellings are placed or arranged auspiciously to benefit spirit beings and life forces and, consequently, the living. Shamans play the classic role of mediating between the worlds, especially between the worlds of the living and their ancestral spirits; these can be bothersome and responsible for a wide range of troubling circumstances in Korea. A shaman would be contracted to journey to the other world to contact them, discover the reason for their restlessness, and placate them, sometimes with food offerings, so they would cease interfering in the daily affairs of their descendants.

Driving the devils out of an old man, Chosen (Korea) Keystone View Company, 1919.

MAGIC

ANOTHER WIDELY DEBATED term in shamanism, "magic" generally means the use of supernatural or unseen power to influence events or alter physical conditions via such means as charms, spells, or magical objects such as magical darts,[67] symbols,[68] a magic pan and magic parrot,[69] magic crystals, magic words, and so on. The use of magic may be of benign or malevolent intent. Some shamans use magic; others do not. The Padlermiut of the Canadian Arctic, for example, did not use magic and disagreed with their neighbors' use of it.

MANDALAS AND MEDICINE WHEELS

BASICALLY, A MANDALA is a geometric form composed of a square within a circle that is frequently divided into four sections. These two forms are then combined with other geometric shapes, such as the triangle and equidistant or four-sided cross. In Buddhist and Hindu symbolism, a mandala represents the wholeness of the universe or perhaps the search for wholeness in an individual. It is also present in the syncretic shamanic/Buddhist Bön tradition of Tibet and in Tantra. A mandala is also a visual representation of sacred sounds or mantras and an expression of vibratory patterns that give form and structure to the physical, material world.

Mandala derives from the Sanskrit, meaning "disk," but the term is now used widely cross-culturally to describe what is viewed as a universal form or combination of forms. The elements of a mandala, as well as its basic form, are found in many spiritual traditions and in many time periods, such as the prehistoric rock art of the Americas.

Among First Nations and Métis of Canada and among Native Americans of the United States, the medicine wheel is an equivalent form to the mandala. Divided into fours, it portrays the circle of life and its transitions such as the four seasons, the four life stages, and so on.

Science suggests that such elemental forms and patterns are due to the architecture of the human brain's neural network.[70]

SEE ALSO: **BUDDHISM; ROCK ART; SACRED GEOMETRY; TANTRA; TIBETAN BÖN OR BON**

MAPS OF THE spirit world help the shaman to navigate the other world in an altered state of consciousness, ensuring success in both entering the Upper or Lower Worlds and, most important, finding their way back. Maps drawn on the front of some Sami drums indicate the three levels along with the entry points that enable the shaman to move back and forth between the worlds. The Tsaatan reindeer-herder shaman Haltsan uses a map that shows the sacred river of his homeland as well as grazing areas for the reindeer on which the Tsaatan rely. In another part of the world, maps that outline the geography of ayahuasca visions are remarkably consistent from one shaman or journey to another, indicating that these are places that are not simply imagined.

SEE ALSO: **AYAHUASCA; JOURNEY, SHAMANIC; TSAATAN REINDEER HERDERS**

IN MANY PARTS of the world, masks are worn by shamans when they journey. Masks may range from simple cloth coverings that hide the face to elaborately detailed carvings of particular animals or birds with moving parts. The latter might be made by accomplished artists or perhaps by shamans themselves. They may be life-sized or miniatures. In their masks, shamans may represent their guardian spirits, ancestors, or various creatures to assist them on their journey; thus, many shamans' masks include feathers to effect flight into the other worlds. Some masks are individualized to a particular shaman; others are cultural archetypes that may be worn by different people at different times or belong to a particular society within a culture. By donning a mask, the wearer assimilates the character and behavior of the subject of the mask, merging with it for the duration of the ritual. Masks are not simply inanimate objects but actually embody the spirit, deity, or being that they represent; they have power in and of themselves. When they're not used in rituals, masks may be kept out of sight in a special place so their power doesn't dissipate or harm others.

SEE ALSO: **MERGING**

This Dorset mask was carved from driftwood and painted. It originally had a fur mustache and eyebrows attached with pegs. The mask was preserved because of the artcic permafrost, which kept it frozen until it was excavated by archaeologist Guy Mary-Rousselière. Shamans probably wore the masks in rituals for curing the sick, controlling the weather, or influencing the hunt. Mask, Late Dorset, Circa A.D. 500-1200. Canadian Museum of History, PfFm-1:1773, S90-3695.

MEDICINE MAN, MEDICINE WOMAN

IN THE ANTHROPOLOGICAL and lay literature, these terms are used interchangeably with "shaman." But especially today, where shamanic traditions have been suppressed or eliminated by dominant cultures or religions, the term "shaman" is no longer used, although medicine men and women may assume the shamans' healing role.

MERGING

A SHAMAN COMBINES forces with their helping spirit such that they become one, bringing together Non-Ordinary Reality and Ordinary Reality. Merging gives the spirit a physical presence in this world while the shaman embodies the power of their helper and may even show their helper's personality or characteristics. When merged, a shaman may move, sound, or even look like their helping spirit—stepping like a heron, making the guttural sounds of a bear, or showing the fierce visage of an ancestor.

Unlike other "spirit" experiences such as possession, merging in the shamanic sense is mutual; that is, carried out with permission of both parties, and it is purposeful or intentional, with a deliberate goal. It is also finite, bounded within clear parameters of coming together and disengaging. And it is of limited duration.

Spirits are a lot like shamans, and some of them may have been shamans! Sometimes they must be courted; sometimes they are temperamental. There are many ways in which spirits are called in; burning sacred plants, drumming, rattling, singing or humming, gifting, dressing and masking, consuming special food or drink, speaking magic words, and stepping through a portal or gateway are among the common ones.

Spirits need shamans as much as shamans need spirits: through the shaman, spirits influence Ordinary Reality, whereas shamans need spirits to help with a wide variety of worldly problems.

At the 1999 International Conference on Shamanism,[71] held in Moscow, Russia, the Buryat shaman Bair Rinchinov merged with the spirit of his grandfather.[72]

Bair Rinchinov was accompanied by his helpers—a man and a woman—who started the fire, dressed him, purified his drum and other paraphernalia in the smoke, drummed throughout the journey, and otherwise assisted. The audience gathered around the fire in a circle and were guided in what to do by his helpers and by other shamans attending the conference. We were told: "The shaman will be summoning the spirit of his grandfather who was 9th generation shaman. His spirit is 110 years old. When spirit enters the shaman's body, try to be silent but to help him, you can pray for him by standing up and putting your three fingers to your brow. Then it is possible to ask questions about your problems." One person who asked for help was a shaman who received, she recounted later, a message and blessing from the grandfather. Bair Rinchinov explained later that he has no recollection of events from the time the spirits join him until they leave: "During the time spirit is in me, I don't know what is said, who comes . . . I find this out from my assistants afterwards."

The moment when the spirit enters the shaman's body is pivotal. We were told to be silent (earlier we had been told we could not videotape during this time). To participate fully and enhance the merging, we could "pray," that is, focus and keep good thoughts in our minds. During the merging, Bair Rinchinov lost awareness or consciousness of himself as a separate being, and physically, he took on the appearance of a very old man.

Bair Rinchinov, hereditary shaman from the Buryat-Aginsk region of Siberia, after conducting a shamanic journey. His mask shows the "eyes" needed to see in the dark, 1999.

MIDDLE WORLD

THE MIDDLE WORLD of the shamanic tripartite universe is the physical or material world of the living. Shamans journey to the Upper or Lower Worlds to seek help for the problems in this, the Middle World. The Sami of northern Europe show "holes" on their drums as access points from the Middle World into the other world. Others ride a horse or enter via a hole in the ground, the roots of a tree, and so on. Solutions to problems in the Middle World are sought in the Upper and Lower Worlds, but there can also be spirits in the Middle World—benign and malevolent—such as ghosts or other beings that did not pass properly upon death.

SEE ALSO: **SAMI; UNDERWORLD OR LOWER WORLD; UPPER WORLD**

MIRROR

The Tuvan shaman and throat singer Nikolay Oorzhak wears a shaman's mirror over his chest to reflect unwanted energies back to the sender, 2004.

IN MANY PARTS of the world, mirrors are used for protection to ward off negative influences or unwelcome hostile spirits. Sometimes they are used for divination to see into the past or the future. Mirrors made of bronze go far back in the archaeological record in places such as China, Italy, India, Mongolia, and Siberia.

SEE ALSO: **DIVINATION**

MONGOLIA

HISTORICALLY, MONGOLIA IS divided into two parts: Inner and Outer Mongolia. Inner Mongolia is in China; Outer Mongolia, known as Mongolia, is a sovereign state in Asia with a complicated history with Russia, China, and the Russian republic of Tuva. Mongolia's constitution provides for freedom of religion, which is dominated by Mongolian Buddhism (heavily influenced by Tibetan Buddhism) and by Mongolian shamanism as the Indigenous folk tradition that Mongolia traces back to the beginning of recorded history. Shamanism has become a symbol today of Mongolian autonomy.

Buddhism and shamanism in Mongolia have, at times, been in conflict, and they have also intermingled. Shamanism blended with Buddhism is called yellow shamanism, whereas shamanism that is not influenced by Buddhism is called black shamanism.[73] For black shamanists, a shaman communicates directly with their spirit, or *ongon,* and there is a Guardian Heaven that takes care of all beings—humans, plants, and animals—in what is called the Sunny World. Yellow shamanists took on Buddhist ideas about world creation and honor *ongod* through Buddhist idols or effigies. *Ongon* (singular; plural, *ongod*) is a symbolic image of a deceased shaman's spirit[74] and as such is a reference to the role of the ancestors in some shamanic lineages.

As a nomadic herding culture, Mongolians rely on five main domestic animals: sheep, camels, yaks, goats, and horses—the horse being the most defining of Mongolian identity. Its horse culture is celebrated as the reason for Mongolia's autonomy and for the unparalleled success of Genghis Khan, also known as Chinggis Khaan, who died in 1227. On horseback, he unified disparate peoples to create the largest contiguous land-based empire the world has ever known. Mongolians say that Genghis Khan relied on the advice of a shaman for his success or was even a shaman himself. The Mausoleum of Genghis Khan is an important center for followers of Mongolian shamanism, and Mongolia has named its main airport after him—Chinggis Khaan International Airport.

A common sight in Mongolia is the *ovoo*, which combines shamanist and Buddhist practices. Built from piles of rocks and a pole or tree branch and then hung with Buddhist prayer flags, they mark the transition between valleys and other places of significance. Offerings are made to the spirits of the place to ensure safe passage for travelers. Offerings might be Buddhist prayer flags, a stone to be added to the pile, or other objects of significance, but some *ovoos* have become places to deposit plastic water bottles or bits of waste. It's a tradition to circumambulate three times around the base of an *ovoo*; our driver drove his van around three times while beeping the horn, ostensibly to wake up the spirits.

An ovoo at sunset on a mountaintop in Mongolia, 2007.

In Mongolia, my fieldwork was mainly with the peoples of the Darhad Valley, who are ethnic Mongolians, and with the Tsaatan reindeer herders, who are ancestrally Tuvan and recent migrants to the region. The Mongolian shaman Galsan Tschinag is of Tuvan ancestry, although he was born in Mongolia in the early 1940s. Under the oppressive regime of Communism, by which Tuvans were scattered, he became a storyteller in the Tuvan tradition and the chief of Tuvans in Mongolia, leading them back to their ancestral homeland in the Altai Mountains. He is the author of more than 30 books; *The Blue Sky* is a novel about the Tuvan nomadic tradition clashing with the pressures of modernity.

SEE ALSO: **TSAATAN REINDEER HERDERS**

Tsaatan reindeer herder and Darhad shamans at a festival in Mongolia, 2006.

The Darhad woman shaman, Odkhu, playing her mouth harp; she is demonstrating how she uses it to journey, 2007.

MOUTH HARP, JEW'S HARP, JAW'S HARP

THE MOUTH HARP, also called a Jew's harp or jaw's harp, is a single-reed musical instrument of ancient origin. Some were found recently in Siberia's Altai Republic and dated to about 1,700 years ago. Apparently made by splintering the ribs of cows or horses, one of them could still hold a tune.

Found in many parts of the world, made of many different materials, and played in a variety of ways, they are sometimes made by skilled craftspersons. In Southeast

Asia, mouth harps are made of bamboo. In Siberia today, they are forged from metal. Both makers and players are highly regarded, so much so that the mouth harp, called *khomus* in Siberia, has become the national instrument of the Sakha Republic, Russia, while a mouth harp museum has been established in *Yakutsk*, its capital city.

Historically in Siberia, especially during the purges of Joseph Stalin, shamans' drums were confiscated as the source of their power. Instead, shamans used the mouth harp to connect with their spirits because it was small, quiet, and easily concealed, but its rhythmic resonance allowed for shamanizing.

The instrument, which is small and portable, is placed against the teeth and then activated in different ways such as by drumming the fingers against the reed. The player breathes into it, and the mouth acts as a sound box. Only one note will be produced, but this can be varied as the player changes the shape of the mouth and by different placements of the tongue.

MOZART, WOLFGANG AMADEUS (1756–1791)

AUSTRIAN MUSICIAN AND composer Wolfgang Amadeus Mozart may seem an odd entry for a book on shamanism, but his story sheds light on the relationship of shamanism to the West. Gloria Flaherty's book *Shamanism and the Eighteenth Century* describes the first encounters of the West with the peoples and practices of shamanism. The 18th century, known as the Age of Reason, combined elements of Enlightenment thinking. European exploration and colonization were at their height. Expeditions to many parts of the world hitherto unknown to the West involved botanists, biologists, missionaries, anthropologists, and other travelers who brought back reports of different places and cultures, including of shamans who could cure, heal, and comfort in ways the West could not explain or sometimes match.

It was also a century when the word "shaman" came to describe a seemingly universal phenomenon in English as well as in other languages.

As a seven-year-old virtuoso, Mozart became a sensation and gradually became known throughout the world as "the living Orpheus," the figure from mythology whom the 18th century considered "the shaman par excellence."[75] And he was compared to other shamans with whom those in the 18th century had become familiar. His talents were considered to be almost supernatural at the time; some considered him to have healing powers. He was thought to be able to transfer power from the realm of the divine to the mundane[76] as shamans are known to do. The German writer and statesman Johann Wolfgang von Goethe (1749–1832) compared Mozart's genius "to a productive kind of spiritual power capable of controlling the hidden animistic forces operative in the world."[77]

MUSIC

MUSIC IS A key means by which culture is preserved, expressed, and passed on, and music articulates the collective spirit of Indigenous Peoples more than any other carrier of culture. It is said to predate language, allowing one to express things that are too important for mere speech.[78]

Shamans say that a rhythm can attract a god or chase away a hostile god or demon. Music is so essential to shamanic ritual that it's not surprising what science reveals about music and the human brain. Different areas of the brain control different aspects of the body. The motor cortex, for example, controls movement, foot tapping, dancing, and playing an instrument. The cerebellum controls the same movements and is also involved in emotional reactions to music. And the auditory cortex controls the first stages of listening to sounds, the perception and analysis of tones.[79] But the processing of music is distributed throughout the brain, making it a truly universal, holistic, and ecstatic human experience.[80]

The *qeej*, or reed mouth organ, is a traditional instrument of the Hmong of Southeast Asia and is played at weddings, funerals, and New Year's ceremonies for entertainment and also in ceremony. Every note or sound is a spoken Hmong word and so is profoundly interconnected with the Hmong language. When Hmong lose their language, they cannot learn the *qeej* and thus cannot perform the funeral ceremony to send the spirits of the dead to join the ancestors in the afterlife. This Hmong musician is playing the *qeej* at the New Year's festival in 2001. The movements of the feet, which look like dance steps, confuse the spirits of the dead so they cannot follow the sound back to this world.

Shamans may themselves be musicians, as is Tuvan shaman and throat singer Nikolay Oorzhak, who was initiated as a shaman because of his musical virtuosity and his skill in overtone singing, which he uses in healing. In his view, "a song is a spirit that moves through space."[81] Or a musician may be not a shaman but another member of a shamanist culture, as with the Hmong *qeej* player.

Besides the voice, the main instruments used in shamanic cultures are the drum and rattle. Other instruments include the mouth harp, gong, and bell.

The Peruvian whistling vessels of the pre-Columbian time period are another set of instruments with possible shamanic associations. They have no modern counterpart. One of the pots can produce four sounds at a time, and they were intended to be played in ensemble. Instead of producing the overtones of Tuvan and Tibetan throat singing, these pots produce the opposite effect or undertone—a powerful low pitch.[82] The pots, which are about 600 years old, are being reproduced and used today in ceremonies and workshops by various practitioners to alter consciousness as they have been shown to alter brain-wave activity.

SEE ALSO: **DRUM; MOUTH HARP, JEW'S HARP, JAW'S HARP; RATTLES**

MYTHOLOGY AND MYTH

"MYTHOLOGY" IS ANOTHER term that anthropologists have debated, but Joseph Campbell is recognized internationally as its foremost authority.[83] He made mythology his life's work, and although he talks and writes "about" mythology rather than narrowly defining it, his views are profound.

Calling mythology "the song of the universe," "the music of the spheres," and "the song of the imagination, inspired by the energies of the body,"[84] he finds evidence of a spiritual awakening in humans from the earliest times; this awakening, he says, distinguishes humans from animals.

Campbell discusses two different orders of mythology: that of one's individual nature and of the natural world of which each of us is part and that of the specific social group to which we belong. Sometimes these two are in conflict with each other or with that of other individuals and other social groups. But mythology is "a harmonizing force,"[85] integrating the individual with their social group and also integrating the social group into the natural world. The mythological experience, then, becomes the realization that a moment in one's life is a moment of eternity and the experience of the eternal aspect in the temporal. Similarly, Juha Pentikäinen sees mythic time as cyclic; shamanic time also is eternal rather than linear.[86]

Myth, in Campbell's view, is a metaphor for the spiritual potentiality of the human experience. When a myth is in your mind, "you see its relevance to something happening in your own life. It gives you perspective on what's happening to you."[87]

SEE ALSO: **CAMPBELL, JOSEPH**

NEAR-DEATH EXPERIENCE (NDE)

AN EXPANDING LITERATURE and research on near-death experiences by medical doctors, psychologists, anthropologists, neuroscientists, and others is opening up research into ethnomedicine and asking questions about the nature of reality and even about the purpose of life. While there is not agreement on what an NDE actually is and under what circumstances it occurs,[88] some[89] find connections with the classic shamanic initiation whereby an initiate experiences death or dismemberment, after which they are remade or reborn as a shaman.

SEE ALSO: **DEATH AND DYING; DISMEMBERMENT; INITIATION**

NEOSHAMANISM AND NEOSHAMANS

THE TERM "NEOSHAMANISM" refers to new forms of shamanism that may or may not draw on past or traditional practices. It may also refer to a revival of traditional practices, perhaps in a new context as peoples with a shamanic tradition have been relocated or where an ancestral shamanic lineage has been broken. In Russia, for example, the purges by Stalin meant many Siberian shamans were murdered or sent to the infamous gulags as threats to the authority of the state. In northern Canada, it is difficult to find Inuit who will admit to visiting a shaman or to being one because of the suppression of traditional practices by Christianity.

As with many of the terms in this book, the phrase is controversial. Is neoshamanism authentic, or is it a form of cultural appropriation? Another view, however, distinguishes core shamanism from neoshamanism while examining the influence of neoshamanism on Indigenous religions and the effects of Indigenous religions on neoshamanism.[90] Others see the Indigenous resurgence of shamanism in Russia as part of an "ethnic revival in the Fourth World."[91]

Perhaps efforts of Michael Harner and the Foundation for Shamanic Studies to acknowledge and revitalize traditional shamanism along with the interest of the Russian Academy of Sciences in documenting the small Indigenous nations of Russia and the involvement of scholars such as M. B. Kenin-Lobsan in Tuva have led to the practice of naming the newly initiated as neoshamans, especially where their ancestral lineage has been lost or interrupted. Such individuals may have shown signs of the gift of shamanizing or may have attended one of the newly established shaman schools and been guided and initiated by an established shaman.[92]

SEE ALSO: **CHRISTIANITY; HARNER, MICHAEL; SIBERIA**

NEW SCIENCES AND SHAMANISM

WHEREAS CONVENTIONAL SCIENCE and many established religions have discredited shamans and shamanic practices as superstitious, unscientific, and outdated with no relevance to the modern world, the new sciences such as new physics, cognitive science, astrophysics, and even mathematics are corroborating and even drawing on Indigenous practices for insights into "new science" explorations.

Conventional science, for example, dismisses the idea of "spirits" with whom shamans connect and the idea of Non-Ordinary Reality coexisting with the Ordinary Reality of this physical world. Yet scientists are setting out to prove that many parallel universes exist.[93]

Shamans say they travel on the sound of their drum, mouth harp, or voice. Andy Clark, subject of the *New Yorker* article "The Mind-Expanding Ideas of Andy Clark," suggests that "to listen to music is to enter into a larger cognitive system comprised of many objects and many people."[94] Clark suggests that the mind is not locked inside us but is "extended," able to expand outward to merge with the things, places, and other minds it thinks with. While shamans are competent in both Ordinary Reality and Non-Ordinary Reality, Clark points out how most of us identify only with our conscious mind. Clark's work helps us understand why Indigenous Peoples claim such a close connection with their homeland and how displacement is so traumatic: "If a person's thought was intimately linked to her surroundings, then destroying a person's surroundings could be as damaging and reprehensible as a bodily attack."[95]

Mathematics has developed a theory to explain hallucinations.[96] The recurrent patterns in cave art—geometric patterns, which appear at the early stages of visual hallucination—provide clues to the circuitry of the brain, reflecting the architecture of the brain's neural network.[97] Such visions, then, are universal, a sort of template, since all human brains share the same template.

Shamanist cultures see themselves as part of nature and their well-being interlinked with the well-being of their lands. Fractals, simply put, are never-ending patterns. By testing the reactions of subjects to viewing fractals found most often in nature (clouds, the spiral of a nautilus shell, and so on), scientists found that physiological and mental stress was reduced by as much as 60 percent, which is far greater than can be achieved pharmacologically.[98]

SEE ALSO: DRUM; INDIGENOUS PEOPLES; MOUTH HARP, JEW'S HARP, JAW'S HARP; MUSIC; SPIRITS

NORTH AMERICA

INDIGENOUS PEOPLES OF North America include Native Americans of the United States as well as First Nations, Inuit, and Métis of Canada. All are traditionally shamanist, but because of religious and government persecution, displacement from traditional lands, and economic, political, and cultural marginalization, many groups no longer use the term "shaman" or describe themselves as shamanist. In some places, spiritual leaders and healers are still called "shamans," but others are called "medicine men" and "medicine women."

A Navajo shaman. Photograph by John K. Hillers, 1872.

At the same time, Indigenous shamanism across North America is undergoing a revival, and people are relying on the accounts of missionaries, travelers, government representatives, anthropologists, and others who documented shamanic practices. Edward S. Curtis (1868–1952), for example, documented what he saw as a disappearing way of life. His photographs, films, and notes perpetuated an influential image of Indigenous Peoples as a "vanishing race." At the same time, they have become invaluable records to those participating in the revival and reclaiming of Aboriginal traditions and spirituality.

Today, Indigenous Peoples are making international connections and finding a common heritage across continents. Peter Gold's 1994 book, *Navajo and Tibetan Sacred Wisdom: The Circle of the Spirit,* documents the many correspondences between these two peoples, although they are far apart geographically. Both, for example, have suffered from colonialism—the colonization of Tibet by China since the 1950s and the Spanish and Anglo-American control over the American Southwest for more than 500 years. Nevertheless, both have retained their spiritual connection with the land that sustains them.

An Inuit shaman, dressed in an elaborate costume, tries to exorcise the evil spirits plaguing a young boy. Library of Congress, c. date unknown.

NORTHWEST COAST CULTURE AREA

THIS IS THE culture area covered by the North Pacific coast of North America and the states and provinces of Alaska, British Columbia, Washington, and Oregon. It includes the Tlingit, Haida, Tsimshian, Tillamook, Salish, and Coast Salish as well as groups known in the literature as Bella Coola, Kwakiutl, and Nootka, although these three groups prefer to be recognized by outsiders as Nuxalk, Kwakwaka'wakw, and Nuu-chah-nulth, respectively.[99] All are traditionally shamanist.

Shamanism of the Northwest Coast has received much attention in the scholarly literature. Waite proposed that Kwakiutl transformation masks originated with human-animal metamorphosis, a classic shamanic experience,[100] while Vastokas related the Northwest Coast totem pole to the shamanic tree of life.[101] These and other examples suggest that shamanic experience provided the basis for many artistic motifs[102] among Northwest Coast cultures. Raven and eagle are two prominent motifs.

SEE ALSO: **AXIS MUNDI**

NUMBERS

THE NUMBER 1 signifies unity, the "oneness" of all of Creation, and the interconnectedness of all life. In the shamanic worldview, all life-forms are sentient beings—humans, plants, rocks, mountains, birds, insects, fish, the wind, and so on.

The Lakota Sioux are credited with the phrase "All My Relations" that has become a common phrase used widely by Indigenous Peoples in North America and elsewhere to recognize that humans and nature are indivisible. Many traditions today use English names such as "Creator," "Great Spirit," or "God," or names in their native language to refer to the "unnameable" One who is the Source of all.

The number 2 signifies the duality of existence, as in, for example, good/evil, light/dark, male/female, seen world/unseen world. This duality of opposites must be kept in balance in order for the universe to operate properly. Some cultures represent the duality as Father Sky/Mother Earth, the sacred union of the cosmos.

The number 3 signifies the tripartite universe comprising the Upper, Middle, and Lower Worlds, which the shaman navigates to provide healing, counseling, and direction in this, the Middle World, and to keep the worlds connected. Some groups expand the levels in the Upper World to multiples of three; some of the Hill Tribes of Southeast Asia, for example, attribute nine levels to their Upper World.

The number 4 is represented as an equidistant cross, the intersection of two pairs of opposites, as in the Tibetan Bön mandalas or the medicine wheel of the Americas. It symbolizes, for example, the four seasons; the four directions; the cycle of life from birth, infancy or childhood through adolescence, into maturity or adulthood, and into old age or death; and so on.

SEE ALSO: **BALANCE, HARMONY; SENTIENCE**

OCEANIA

USE OF THE terms "shaman" and "shamanism" is controversial in the ethnography of Oceania, which includes Australia, New Zealand, Polynesia, and other nearby countries. In Polynesia, for example, are "spirit mediums" who claim to be possessed by spirits shamans or not, since shamans claim to actually visit the spirit world?[103] Some scholars would say no: Shamans must be in control of their spirits, and mediums are not. But scholars change their minds from time to time.

The controversy here and elsewhere centers on which definition of "shaman" and "shamanism" one uses—whether Mircea Eliade's strict definition restricts their uses mainly to Central Asia or whether developments of the past 20 years or so expand the definitions to include a wider geographic and historical area that could include other magico-religious practitioners.

Organizations such as the International Society for Academic Research on Shamanism (ISARS), which continues the work of the International Society for Shamanistic Research (ISSR) and publishes the *Shaman* journal, and the Foundation for Shamanic Studies, which publishes the *Shamanism* journal, continue to debate these very basic questions.

SEE ALSO: **AUSTRALIA AND ABORIGINES; ELIADE, MIRCEA; SHAMAN—DEFINITION AND MEANING; SHAMANISM—DEFINITION AND MEANING**

ORAL HISTORY OR ORAL TRADITION

IN ORAL TRADITIONS, people relate their stories, experiences, and teachings directly from one person to another; thus, they are stored in a collective memory rather than in text. Some groups, however, say their history is written on the land. Others describe how elements of the landscape such as mountains, rivers, berry bushes, and so on, hold their stories.[104] Among the Akha, a Hill Tribe of northern Thailand, the *pima*, or "holder of tradition," can recite Akha history from memory over many hours. With a transition from oral to written history, much is lost, but Indigenous Peoples worldwide are involved in oral history projects to preserve their language, culture, and traditional knowledge.

INSIGHTS INTO THE origins of shamanism and its universalism come from new understandings about the origin of the human species. The Genographic Project, begun in 2005 by the National Geographic Society, mapped the history of human migration patterns through genetic anthropological study—the collection and analysis of DNA samples from modern-day Indigenous populations across the globe.

The results showed that all humans living today are descendants of people who originated in Africa. The spiritual beliefs and practices of the San or !Kung of the Kalahari Desert offer insights into the development of shamanism as a universal tradition with localized expressions. About 40,000 years ago, migrations began out of humanity's ancestral homeland. As groups migrated into other parts of the world, they adapted to changing climatic conditions and differing resources. Adaptations also included physical changes such as lighter skin color to adapt to the colder climates and less sunlight of northern Europe.

Geneticist Spencer Wells mapped migrations from what is now southern Africa northward into Europe, eastward into Asia, east and southward into Australasia, north and eastward into the far north, then across the Bering Sea into North America, and from there southward into South America. New environments and new livelihoods accommodated adaptations of spiritual practices and beliefs. Farming, for example, requires different types of knowledge, a different relationship to land, and thus different rituals than do hunting or fishing.

A different approach suggests a similar common humanity. Mircea Eliade[105] and Joseph Campbell relate how the development of shamanism is not associated with any specific moment in history or with any particular culture or social system. Instead, they point out, shamanism appears to be fundamental to the human condition; its central and defining feature is the ecstatic experience, today termed the "shamanic journey." Campbell writes that "the central nervous system of our species has hardly changed in the mere 12,000 to 15,000 years following the period of the shamans of the caves,"[106] meaning caves of the Upper Paleolithic time period, including the caves of Lascaux. The cave art (increasingly associated by scholars with shamanism) signifies "an interest in sharing knowledge, expressing feelings, and transmitting cultural information to later generations."[107] Herein lie the origins of shamanism.

Paleolithic Period: The earliest period of human development, it lasted until about 8000 BCE and is divided into two time periods:
Lower Paleolithic to c. 40,000 BCE
Upper Paleolithic, c. 40,000–8000 BCE

SEE ALSO: **CAMPBELL, JOSEPH; ELIADE, MIRCEA; JOURNEY, SHAMANIC; ROCK ART**

PAGANISM, PAGAN

THE TERM "PAGANISM" was first used in the fourth century by the early Christian Church to separate its followers from those who did not follow Christ's teachings. As such, it was a derogatory term; however, it was not a term that people used to describe their own religious or spiritual practices, which may have included animism or belief in multiple gods. People did not call themselves pagans until the 20th century, when there developed an interest in reviving religious and cultural practices of the ancient world. Today, neopaganism is often associated with Celtic practices and forms of nature worship. The term "paganism" may be used in association with or even interchangeably with "neoshamanism" in the West, as such terms become more widely used and more inclusive. SEE ALSO: **CELTIC; NEOSHAMANISM AND NEOSHAMANS**

PAYMENT

ALTHOUGH SHAMANS ARE not specialists in that they also have other roles in their families and communities, clients pay something for a shaman's services, depending on the type of service and what is valued in a particular society.

The recipient of the payment and its beneficiaries may be explained differently in different cultural contexts—the shamans may benefit directly, and the spirits that a shaman is appeasing or inviting in may be seen as beneficiaries.

Among the Hmong of Southeast Asia, who are horticulturalists, a sick person or their family pays back the spirit by offering animals—mostly pigs or chickens—gold and silver, paper money, whiskey, or incense.[108] If a chicken or a pig is offered, it is usually shared in a communal meal. And if it is a life-threatening situation, an offering of very high value such as a water buffalo may be offered. In other contexts, money may be offered.

PERSONAL POWER

A SHAMAN'S POWER results from a combination of their personal attributes and abilities and those of their spirit helpers, which may include their ancestors. In a family or group, people will know each other's ancestry and so will know if shamans have strong ancestral spirits or come from a long line of shamans who help them in helping others. Sometimes those ancestral spirits will be cranky or difficult and the shaman will need to be strong to handle them. Chulu, a Tsaatan reindeer herder in northern Mongolia, comes from an ancestral line of shamans, and her children are shamans. But, she told me, she was sick as a child and thus not strong enough to become a shaman herself. Power also comes from the challenges a shaman overcomes, as the initiation of a shaman can be very difficult, requiring physical and mental stamina. And power comes from the various spirit helpers that assist the shaman as needed and may become part of a shaman's toolkit or medicine bag. Amulets, for example, do not just represent power; they embody it. Siberian shamans' dress becomes very heavy as objects are added to signify success with a client. Someone has to be physically strong to be able to bear such a heavy costume, and some give up shamanizing when they become too weak or old to do so.

SEE ALSO: **AMULET; INITIATION**

Chulu, Tsaatan reindeer herder from northern Mongolia and one of my beloved teachers, 2006.

TRADITIONALLY, SHAMANIZING TOOK place in
a shaman's homeland where the ancestors and other
helping spirits reside and from which shamans derive
their power. Today, however, many Indigenous cultures
have been displaced. The ancestral homelands of the
Tsaatan reindeer herders are in Tuva, but they were forced
to relocate to the mountains of northern Mongolia. Now,
because they are recent immigrants, they are said to have
fewer spirits in the Darhad region of Mongolia. In comparison, the neighboring Darhad Mongolians claim that
their ancestry in this region goes back to beyond the time
of Chinggis Khan; thus, the Darhad claim to have more
spirits residing in the valley. On the other hand, Tsaatan
shamans are considered the most powerful by some
because they reside in the mountainous areas where they
are closer to nature.

Buriat shaman Bair Rinchinov described his drum as
"Lake Baikal," the notable feature of his homeland, which
is an obvious reference to the incorporation of "place"
into the shaman's drum. Because spirits reside in particular places of a landscape, shamans say they must ask the
spirits for permission when traveling to shamanize in a
new place; otherwise, such spirits may be offended (and
sometimes do not give their permission).

Today, shamans are traveling "away" to participate in
festivals, conferences, and other gatherings; to instruct in
schools or initiate neoshamans; or to work with international clients. For some, it is controversial as to whether
shamans should shamanize outside their homeland and
whether they should take their spirits with them. The
Mongolian shaman Maamaa is called a "real" shaman by
his neighbors because he will not travel "away," whereas
the Tsaatan shaman Haltsan described that at an event
for outsiders such as tourists, it would be disrespectful

for him to call in all of his spirit helpers. Others don't call in their spirits at all if they are doing a demonstration or performing for tourists.

SEE ALSO: **MONGOLIA; NEOSHAMANISM AND NEOSHAMANS; TSAATAN REINDEER HERDERS**

PLANTS

WHETHER SHAMANS USE plants to any extent depends on their personal qualities and interests and perhaps also on their ancestral spirits and the kind of knowledge they had when they were living. Certainly, plant use is not the sole prerogative of shamans. Anyone might use plants for medicinal or spiritual purposes, but some may be known for their extensive knowledge.[109]

The time of year to harvest, which parts of the plant to use in what combination, whether to use them dry or fresh ... these are all considerations in using plants for healing. Many ethnobotany projects have documented plant knowledge in Indigenous and shamanic cultures. I asked Ludmilla in Siberia about which plants she used for medicine: "All plants are medicinal," she replied. "You just have to know how to use them." Jeorgina Larocque, Mi'kmaq medicine woman from Nova Scotia, Canada, harvests by the Rule of Seven: "I never take the mother plant and never more than one out of every seven offspring. That way I leave enough for the next seven generations."

Tsaatan reindeer herder Chulu speaks about sustainable ways to harvest and the holistic use of the medicinal plant *Wansemberuu* (*Saussurea* species), which grows in the far reaches of the mountains and is difficult to get to on horseback or even on a reindeer. Global warming is devastating its habitat, and it is being overharvested as people come up from the city because they have heard of this plant and its healing properties or just want it as a curiosity.

Chulu speaks about when the plant is most beneficial—
before the plant puts its energy into seed production
and at the time of year when the sun is highest in the sky
and infusing the plant with its energy. She doesn't cut
the flower from its stem or dig up the root; instead she
uses it in situ, taking the sick person to the flower on a
sort of pilgrimage. Thus, the plant itself is not destroyed.
If the sick person were an adult, the difficulties of making
the journey would show intent to get better. Where it is
a baby who is sick, effort shows what the healer is willing
to do on the child's behalf. Gradually, the plant changes
the baby's vibration, bringing the child back to wellness.

 There is a flower called Wansemberuu which grows up
on the far mountains, especially on the east taiga. On
some mountains, it's very rare. We use it in many ways . . .
I only visit it from June 20 to July 5. So during this period,
the flower hasn't fully bloomed—it's still closed. I don't
collect the flower but I bring people who are sick to the
flower. On top of it are drops of dew, drops of moisture.
My father used to tell me, don't use all the dew, just
one drop . . . The first time, I used a spoon and it was
difficult, but the second time, I drew the water up with
a syringe and gave it to my son—not even one year
old. That winter my son got cold and his lungs were
bad and his voice sounded bad. I took my son three
times to that flower, once a day. After three visits, my
father told me, 'Now your son's going to be good.'"

Next, her father made soup from a freshly killed
reindeer. Mostly, the Tsaatan rely on milk products
from their reindeer, and wealth has traditionally been
measured by the number of reindeer in their herds.
A reindeer would be killed only on a special occasion
such as this one, to bring a sick child back to health.

Reindeer forage widely (when they can), eating a variety of plants from the forest and the tundra, from the streams and the mountains—all these "medicines" the reindeer eat depending on what they need to stay healthy. So all the medicines from the Tsaatan homelands are available to those who consume reindeer milk and, as needed, reindeer meat.

> Then my father killed a reindeer and made fresh soup for my son. He took a bit of every part of the reindeer, put all the bits into the intestines and boiled them. My father told me, 'You've got to give him this. I gave him soup, to my son, and little bits of meat. I cut it up really small and gave it to him off a spoon. My son got better and is grown."[110]

All parts of the animal were used and contained in the broth so none of the goodness was lost. When Chulu fed tiny bits of meat and spoonfuls of the broth to her baby, she was feeding him bits of the land— its plants, animals, and the people who cared for it. She was feeding him bits of her community—and its spirit—that nurtured her child, herself, her father, and the ancestors before them.

Chulu's granddaughter moving camp with the family's reindeer, 2006.

PORTALS AND PATHWAYS

PORTALS ARE OPENINGS or entries into the Upper and Lower Worlds of the shamanic cosmos. They take forms such as doorways, gates, bridges, arches, or holes. On the surface of Sami drums, for example, drawn holes between the three levels are "the manifestation of the outstanding capacity of the shaman to wander from zone to zone and to interact with the deities and the spirits of each zone where necessary."[111] At the portal, the shaman may need to use certain rituals or incantations to affect an opening or shout loudly to attract the attention of beings on the other side.

A pathway might be a tree, a river, a ladder, ropes, or something else that leads to the portal, or the pathway itself might be the actual entry into the other worlds. A shaman may travel on the beat of a drum or the sound of a horse's hooves, on a horse itself, on the rhythm of a rattle or mouth harp, or via the smoke of a sacred plant or sacred fire to reach the other world.

Such entries must be kept open by the shaman so that this world and the other world remain as one, each engaged and interdependent with the other. Today, shamans say that humanity is "dispirited" and that the world is in trouble because the portals between the worlds have closed.

SEE ALSO: **DRUM; HORSE; RATTLE; SAMI**

POSTURES, SHAMANIC

DRAWING ON ARCHAEOLOGICAL finds, prehistoric art, rock art, and other representations of shamans inducing trance or journeying, Felicitas Goodman suggests that particular postures facilitate the shamanic journey.[112] Such postures—seated, seated on a stool, standing, lying, kneeling, or kneeling on one knee—are found cross-culturally, with each posture appearing to create a consistent experience. Some take one "to the sky" and even beyond, others to the Middle World where humans reside, and others to the Lower World. Such postures may be seen in the image of a shaman in the caves of Lascaux, for example, which can be replicated by lying down on a board positioned at a 37-degree angle. Or in the "Bear Spirit" posture, which is "extremely old and the most widely known of all the postures," having endured through time from classical Egypt to the Aztec empire to modern-day Siberia. Goodman says the posture is so powerful that a carving or other representation can be used in some folk traditions to "mediate a cure if the patient is too ill or weak to assume it" themselves.

Some postures were apparently designed to facilitate metamorphosis, that is, shapeshifting or changing between human and nonhuman form. Goodman's studies show how divination and other shamanic techniques are best achieved in trance and in the appropriate posture to facilitate a particular outcome. Surely the yogic positions or asanas are a development of archaic shamanic experience.

SEE ALSO: **SHAPESHIFTING**

Neoshaman Roman Nesterov demonstrating shaman's flying stones at a Siberian archaeological site, 1999.

POWER ANIMALS

POWER ANIMALS ARE animal spirit helpers who assist the shaman in navigating the two realities, although others besides shamans may have power animals. A person may even be protected by a power animal without being aware of it.[113] They are always benevolent to their human, although a shaman or sorcerer may use them to cause harm to others, especially when protecting themselves or their family or group. Power animals are almost universally wild rather than domesticated, and if you make a connection with a power animal such as an eagle, you have the protection and guidance of the entire species. Some shamans keep their power animals a secret; otherwise, they say, they lose power. Others openly wear their power animals on their dress, mask, drum, or rattle. When a shaman is "one" with a power animal and in an ASC, they may make the sounds, movements, or actions of their power animal. With its qualities, they assume the ability to dive into the depths of the ocean or fly into the highest reaches of the sky.

Animals may appear in human form, or humans may metamorphose into an animal to be able to navigate in a realm or in a way that is not ordinary to humans.[114] The deer shown on the deer stones of Central Asia, for instance, transcend this world by assuming the ability of bird flight. For Mircea Eliade, shamans are the last humans able to converse with animals.

SEE ALSO: **DEER STONES; MERGING; SHAPESHIFTING**

In his 1930 book *Intellectual Culture of the Hudson Bay Eskimos* [sic], Knud Rasmussen documented the idea of death and the afterlife among the Padlermiut or Caribou Inuit of the Canadian Arctic and describes the interconnectedness of animals and humans:

The mistress of the animals of the hunt, Pinga, lives somewhere up in the air or in the sky and is often named quite indiscriminately with Hila. She is the guardian of all life, both man and animal, but she does not offer man eternal hunting grounds like the god-head of the coast dwellers; she collects all life on the land itself and makes it eternal solely in this manner, that everything living reappears there.

When an animal or a person dies, the soul leaves the body and flies to Pinga, who then lets the life or the soul rise again in another being, either man or animal. As a rule, there is no fear of death, and I remember that Igjugarjuk would sometimes say half jokingly that he had undoubtedly been so imperfect as a human being that his soul, when it went to Pinga after his death, would only be allowed to rise again as a little burrowing lemming.

PROTECTIVE OR GUARDIAN SPIRITS

A BELIEF IN protective or guardian spirits and the need for them to ensure well-being seems universal, as is the practice of representing them—giving them form and a physical presence. Guardian spirits protect the owner and the owner's surroundings by warding off unwelcome influences, bad spirits, and other intrusions. Guardian spirits also act as a portal or transport into the other world.

Protective spirits are among the many types of spirits that communities or individuals might acquire. Anyone can appeal to their personal protective spirits; however, troubles caused by malevolent spirits would normally be dealt with by shamans.

The form such spirits take differs widely across cultures, from petroglyphs and pictographs to life-sized wooden carvings to tiny dolls that can be carried around in a medicine bag.

The Akhas, one of the Hill Tribes of Southeast Asia, have three types of helping spirits—their own ancestral spirits, the Creator Spirit, and a number of different guardian spirits. Malevolent spirits are generally divided into "inside" and "outside" spirits. At each end of an Akha village are gates that protect "inside" from "outside"—everything inside the gates is a protected area where Akhas live free from negative influences and the dangers of the outside world.[115] In front of each gate are placed two almost life-sized effigies of a woman and a man. There is disagreement about the purpose of these figures, but they may be protecting the inside haven from the dangerous outside.

A black cloth doll from the Konkan region of India is hung at the doorway of a house. As someone enters, it scares away any bad spirits so they're not carried inside.

PSYCHEDELIC SHAMANISM

THE TERM "PSYCHEDELIC" was coined by British doctor Humphry Osmond and suggested at a meeting of the New York Academy of Sciences in 1957. Osmond's early work used psychedelics such as lysergic acid diethylamide (LSD) to treat addiction and to study schizophrenia. He derived the term from the Greek *psyche*, meaning "mind," and *delos*, meaning "manifest"; thus, "mind-manifesting." Psychedelic shamanism explores plants and other substances used in traditional shamanic contexts or in neoshamanism for their mind-manifesting properties.

While traditional cultures would have used such substances in situ, from locally available sources, and with cultural protocols and rituals, neoshamanism may draw on such knowledge and experience but integrate them into a new context, perhaps developing new rituals to suit such a context and its participants. Traditional users, sometimes shamans, may be imported to lead a group, or outsiders may travel to a traditional context or community.

The Multidisciplinary Association for Psychedelic Studies (MAPS), founded in 1986 by Rick Doblin, is a nonprofit research and educational organization that develops legal, medical, and cultural contexts to benefit people from the scientific study and careful use of marijuana and psychedelics. Its research includes clinical trials of MDMA-assisted psychotherapy for post-traumatic stress disorder (PTSD), published in the peer-reviewed journal *Psychopharmacology*. Its *Psychedelic Bibliography* provides a comprehensive overview of psychedelics research, including a complete listing of studies on the therapeutic use of psychedelics from 1931 to 1995 as well as recently published research.

SEE ALSO: **NEOSHAMANISM AND NEOSHAMANS**

PSYCHIC POWERS

MANY PSYCHIC POWERS have been identified and named by Western science and metaphysics, such as divination, dowsing, bilocation (the ability to be in two locations simultaneously), levitation (the ability to float or fly by mystical means), and precognition (the ability to perceive future events).

Though such powers are not restricted to shamans, shamans will attribute them to their union with the spirit world and sometimes to particular spirit helpers. Eagle, for example, has "farsightedness"—it can see small details from a great distance. With eagle as ally, a shaman might navigate Non-Ordinary Reality in search of lost items, to locate the source of a problem in the past or the future, or to locate a lost soul part.

It is interesting how science now acknowledges that humans have many more senses than the commonly accepted five of sight, sound, smell, touch, and taste; we have at least 21 senses, possibly more.[116] Science is corroborating what shamans have known for millennia.

SEE ALSO: **DIVINATION**

PSYCHOPATHOLOGY

PSYCHOPATHOLOGY IS THE scientific study of mental disorders. Research in clinical and laboratory settings by psychologists, psychiatrists, neuroscientists, and others is aimed at understanding the many manifestations of mental disorder. Although the science is continually evolving, it attributes mental disorders to psychological, genetic, biological, and social causes. On the other hand, shamanist traditions view such disorders as disorders of the spirit. Individuals or entire groups can become "dispirited," suffering from soul or spirit loss; thus, depression, anxiety, dissociation, and other conditions manifest. It is encouraging to see that in many countries now, shamans work with healthcare professionals in Western medicine to explore psychopathology from a broader perspective.

PSYCHOPOMP

A PSYCHOPOMP IS a person who assists or accompanies souls or spirits to cross over to the other world. The term comes from the Greek word *psukhopompos* or *psykhopompos* (from *psukhē* or *psykhē*, meaning "soul, mind, spirit," and *pompos*, meaning "guide" or "conductor"). In Greek mythology, it refers to a guide or conductor of souls to the place of the dead or the afterworld.

In neoshamanism, the term is used to mean "spirit guide." A shaman acting as psychopomp guides the deceased to make the transition from this world to the afterlife. Or a shaman may accompany a troublesome spirit with whom a client has become codependent to the Upper or Lower World where the spirit will be "happier."[117] Sometimes one or the other is reticent to make the transition.

This is potentially dangerous work as the spirit could transfer from client to shaman. As with any shamanic venture, a practitioner needs to be power-filled and experienced.

RATTLES

RATTLES CONTRIBUTE TO the multisensory experience of shamanic ritual. A rattle may be handheld or may attach to the wrist or ankle. Metal or bone bits, bells, or small animal hooves may be attached to the back of a drum or to the shaman's dress to create percussive sound when the drum is beaten or the shaman moves. As with drums, rattles come in many forms and are made of many different materials.

The rain stick of the Americas is made from a hollow cactus stem from which the spines are first removed and then tapped into the cavity. Small stones are dropped in, and the ends are sealed. When the rain stick is inverted, the stones falling through the spines sound like rain. A rattle from New Mexico uses tiny bits of gravel thrown up around the entrance to an anthill; these are collected and dropped into a rawhide bulb, giving this particular rattle "ant energy."

REVIVAL OF SHAMANISM

IN ALL PARTS of the world, shamanism is undergoing a revival or renaissance as many individuals and organizations advocate for greater recognition of traditional healing principles and practices. And we are seeing its integration with conventional medicine as a holistic approach to healing and wellness, both curative and preventive. Many countries now have traditional healers working alongside Western doctors and mental health experts in hospitals and clinics, providing complementary medical care for Indigenous patients—especially those recovering from the intergenerational trauma of colonization—and also for others who recognize its benefits.

Non-Indigenous people are increasingly interested in traditional healing as they search for alternatives to mainstream models of physical and mental health. Western medicine has marginalized Indigenous medicine as ethnomedicine. They differ in many ways, but essentially, Western medicine views the body from a mechanistic perspective with each part treated separately. Psychiatrists deal with problems of the mind and medical doctors with problems of the body, but further divisions occur into specialties of the heart, skin, muscles, and so on. In comparison, traditional medicine is holistic, recognizing the interconnectedness of all life and connecting people to their culture, their communities (past and present), and their homelands.

At the same time, shamans and other Indigenous healers are adapting to new circumstances and new environmental pressures. Administering to patients from different backgrounds or working in urban and international settings brings its own challenges. Ancestral shamanic lineages are being revived and new ones established where shamanism has been suppressed. And Indigenous Peoples are working across cultural boundaries to form alliances to keep their traditions alive and to represent their interests with a strong collective voice.

RITUAL AND CEREMONY

RITUALS, SOMETIMES CALLED ceremonies, are intentional activities undertaken in a prescribed or customary way for a specific purpose and in a sacred context; thus, they have a beginning and an end. Some people use the words "ritual" and "ceremony" interchangeably, as I do here, while others define "ceremony" as a ritual performed on a single occasion. Some rituals are restrictive as to who may attend and how to behave; others are more open, but such protocols depend on the particular culture and who conducts the ritual.

Shamanic ritual might include cleansing and purification, psychopomp work, divination, exorcism or extraction, sacrifice, initiation of another shaman, commemorative occasions such as the birth of a child, rites of passage, or what anthropologist Victor Turner calls "rites of affliction"—actions that seek to mitigate spirits that inflict humans with misfortune.

Ritual objects may be involved—masks or particular items of clothing, plants, feathers, a drum or rattle, daggers, headdresses, and so on. Fire, smoke, or water may be involved. Sometimes a cleansing and purification will be conducted at the beginning or a sacred drink shared at the end. Rituals connect participants with one another and, in a sacred context, with the beings that inhabit the other worlds.

Tuvan shaman performing a ritual to call in the rain because the weather had been dry and the crops suffered, 2001.

SEE ALSO: **DIVINATION; EXTRACTION, EXORCISM; FIRE; MASKS; PSYCHOPOMP**

ROCK ART

ROCK ART REFERS to human-made marks on natural rock and stone surfaces, including the faces of mountains, cliffs, and cave walls. It includes petroglyphs, which are carved into the rock surface, and pictographs, which are drawn or painted on the rock surface with red ochre, charcoal, minerals such as manganese, chalk, or even blood. "Parietal art" is the particular term archaeologists use for cave art—human-made drawings, paintings, etchings, and carvings—made on the interior walls of caves and rock shelters.

Rock art is found throughout the world and in places that were isolated geographically or in time and seems to be a universal form of human expression regardless of location or time period. While the original meanings of the work are lost in time, many researchers are working with living Indigenous Peoples including present-day shamans to interpret the meaning; however, interpreting rock art as shamanic or even magico-religious is still controversial among academics.

The oldest-known rock art dates from the Upper Paleolithic time period of 50,000 to 100,000 years ago, having been found in Europe, Australia, Asia, and Africa. Among the most famous of known rock art sites are the European sites about which David Lewis-Williams and Werner Herzog offer newer interpretations. *The Mind in the Cave: Consciousness and the Origins of Art* by archaeologist Lewis-Williams is a 2002 study of Upper Paleolithic European rock art. It offers the shamanistic interpretation of the work as being at the forefront of rock art research, proposing that the explanation lies in the evolution of the human mind. The study suggests that Cro-Magnons, unlike Neanderthals, possessed a more advanced neurological makeup that enabled them to experience shamanistic trance and vivid mental imagery. In his 3-D documentary film *Cave of Forgotten Dreams* (2010), director Herzog also supports the idea of a sudden leap in the development of human consciousness and of a shamanistic intent to the works. On the walls of the Chauvet Cave in southern France, bison, rhinoceroses, mammoths, lions, cave bears, horses, mammoths, and other animals are depicted. Carbon dating places them at between 30,000 and 32,000 years old. Despite their age, however, Herzog sees them as fully accomplished works of art, no less sophisticated than what artists create today. All of a sudden, he says, "we have the presence of what I would call 'the modern human soul.'"[118]

Pictograph from Sego Canyon in East Central Utah showing a horned figure that may be a shaman in SSC; the rock face shows some defacement, 2007.

In the American Southwest, tens of thousands of petroglyphs and pictographs have been found in many different locations. Some are hidden away in hard-to-reach places, while others are situated prominently and are easy to access. Light-colored rock was usually chosen for the pictographs of this area to enhance their visibility. Carbon dating reveals a range of dates of Southwest rock art with some going back to 5500 BCE.[119] Many sites that are out in the open have been damaged over the years by vandalism, construction, and natural weathering, but many have been documented. More attention is being paid to conservation, protection, and education about their value as irreplaceable heritage sites. Again, interpretations vary, but the association of rock art with shamanism is becoming more accepted.

SACRED GEOMETRY REFERS to the study of archetypal patterns of which the material world is composed and that are core patterns of creation. Similarly, shamanist cosmology is based on underlying "core" principles that are universal cross-culturally. Mircea Eliade, for example, views shamanic traditions in sacred relationship with the cosmos and the world as the work of Supernatural Beings—a divine work and hence sacred in its very structure.[120] In Indigenous cultures that have not been transformed by colonization and religious conversion, songs, stories, artwork, homes, a shaman's dress—all such cultural elements refer to this sacred structure. Shamans themselves are human/nature merged, embodying the integration of physical and spiritual, of this worldliness and otherworldliness.[121]

Two young Hmong girls from northern Thailand wearing their traditional dress at Hmong New Year's celebrations in 2001. A new set of clothes is made every new year. By re-creating their characteristic patterns, the sewer re-creates the Hmong universe.

SEE ALSO: **CORE SHAMANISM; COSMOLOGY AND COSMOGONY**

THE SAMI (ALSO spelled *Sámi* or *Saami*) inhabit northern parts of Norway and Sweden, northern parts of Finland, and part of Russia. Known historically as Lapps or Laplanders, they are shamanist by tradition. Many are now Christianized but retain elements of their shamanic past while participating in a contemporary shamanic revival. Juha Pentikäinen, writing about contemporary Sami and Siberian shamans who survived Soviet exile and the persecutions of the Stalin regime, suggests that attention should be given to the visible elements of shamanism as well as to "its latent meanings and esoteric messages."[122] These come together in the front, public, or collective side of the shaman's drum with the back private. The drum is such an important part of a shaman's toolkit in this region, he calls it the shaman's "liturgical handbook" and a cognitive map.[123]

Sami drums have fascinated outsiders for centuries. In the 17th and 18th centuries, hundreds of drums were exported to Europe by explorers and missionaries. One drum went to the Grand Duke of Tuscany along with a boy sent along to show him how to play it. A Sami drum traditionally was three-part: the drum itself; the beater, wand, or hammer; and the ring. Together they formed a whole. Here Paolo Mantegazza gives a description of the three parts:

To ask advice before any undertaking of some importance (a journey, a hunting or fishing trip) or in a case of illness, the Lapp [Sami] consulted the *runebom*. It seems that every family had one, just as every Protestant family has a Bible. Only in the case of more serious matters the *noaidi* was asked to act as an intermediary: normally the *runebom* was consulted by the head of the family. After numerous preparations and gesticulations the vuorbe [the ring] was placed on the drum, which was then beaten by the wand until the bouncing ring was finally stopped on some figure and refused to move away from it. The place where the ring had stopped revealed the will of the gods."[124]

THE SAN

SCHOLARS DIFFER AS to definitions of shamanism and whether it can be applied to anywhere in Africa. Swedish ethnologist Äke Hultkrantz (1920–2006) agrees with Mircea Eliade's view of shamanism as universal and applying to all continents "with the possible exceptions of Africa and Australia."[125]

One group, the San, however, is given special mention here. Rituals in southern Africa go back at least 70,000 years, the earliest known evidence in the world. The date is based on an archaeological find of a cave site in Botswana discovered in researching the origin of the San,[126] also known as the !Kung. The San's ancestors are believed to be the first inhabitants of Botswana and South Africa. *The Journey of Man*[127] traces the African diaspora out of what is now southern Africa by analyzing the genetic evidence of the Y chromosome; the journey began about 50,000 years ago and then populated all parts of the globe.

The San retain the world's oldest healing and spiritual traditions and are widely known for their shaking medicine, an improvised and spontaneous healing trance dance into which healers go to cure sickness—physical or psychological. We can learn from them about the "original" shaman.[128]

SCAPULIMANCY

OF THE MANY types of divination used in shamanism, scapulimancy uses bones. One type of scapulimancy, practiced in East Asia and North America, involves putting an animal's scapula (its triangular-shaped shoulder blade) into a specially prepared and very hot fire, where it blackens and cracks. The shaman then reads the cracks and uses them, for example, to divine the location of a lost or stolen article or to predict the outcome of a venture such as a battle.

SEE ALSO: **DIVINATION**

SECRET LANGUAGE

WHEN IN AN altered state, a shaman may speak in a language quite different from that used in everyday speech; it may be unknown to participants in a ceremony other than the shaman and their helpers. It may be the language of animal spirit helpers—some shamans are known to be able to speak with the animals—or the language of the ancestors. For example, Jeorgina Larocque, Mi'kmaq medicine woman from Nova Scotia, Canada, communicates with her grandmother in the spirit world via a secret "old" language that is not spoken today.

SENTIENCE

TO BE SENTIENT means to be conscious, to be able to perceive and feel. Science has come to show that animals such as elephants and wolves are sentient, and most of us today accept that animals are able to experience emotions and sensations and to form attachments. But in the shamanic universe, all of Creation is sentient. Thus, everything in the natural world is conscious: Trees, plants, animals, birds, and even stones and rocks, rivers, the wind, rain, and thunder, along with humans, are sentient beings worthy of human respect and care.

SHAKING MEDICINE

SHAKING MEDICINE IS a traditional technique of the San of the Kalahari Desert in southern Africa and the oldest shamanic healing tradition in the world.[129] Ecstatic shaking of the human body produces the transcendent state necessary for profound healing. In writing about the San, Bradford Keeney examines how the alternating of ecstatic arousal with deep trance relaxation brings all the body's energetic systems into balance; they then produce the shaking medicine that supports embodiment of the universal life force and, ultimately, spiritual attunement.

Shaking for therapeutic benefit is also practiced by the Shakers and Quakers of the United States as well as in India, Japan, and the Caribbean, among other places. Today, trauma release exercises (TRE) assist the body in releasing deep muscular patterns of stress and tension, and calming down the nervous system. All assist in physiological release. San shaking medicine, however, invokes the world of Spirit.

SEE ALSO: **BALANCE, HARMONY; THE SAN**

SHAKING TENT

ACROSS NORTH AMERICA, shamanic power was publicly demonstrated in the widespread shaking tent ceremony that is still practiced today in the Innu, Naskapi, and Cree traditions,[130] though in modified form; it was also common among the Ojibwa, Innu (Montagnais-Naskapi), Cree, Penobscot, and Abenaki.[131] While in Nova Scotia several years ago, I witnessed the shaking tent occur spontaneously during a sweat lodge with Emile Gautreau, a Métis Mi'kmaq medicine man.

Traditionally, a shaman entered the specially constructed tent for a variety of reasons, among them: to make contact with people some distance away, to wage battle with other shamans and sorcerers, to cure and heal, and to make direct contact with the Animal Masters to locate game and ask for help in hunting.[132]

The earliest report of the shaking tent ceremony came from Jesuit missionary Father Paul LeJeune during his winter stay of 1633 to 1634 among the Montagnais of Labrador and Quebec in Canada. As in other accounts of the time, "shaman" is referred to as "juggler" and the prejudices of the writer will be apparent. He assumed, for instance, that the shaman was making the tent shake and that the shaman was imitating the voices of spirits, contrary to the views of the Montagnais.

SHAMAN—DEFINITION AND MEANING

AS WITH MANY of the terms in this book, there is controversy about the meaning of the word "shaman" and its origin. The word "shaman" is said by some authorities to have come from the Tunguso-Manchurian *šaman* and from the Sanskrit *śramana* by way of China, meaning "Buddhist monk." Joseph Campbell proposes a different etymology of *šaman*, a noun, derived from *ša*, a Tunguso-Manchurian verb meaning "to know." Thus, a shaman is "one who knows."[133] Touraj Daryaee, on the other hand, gives it a pre-Siberian origin.

Though once applied strictly to Central Asia, the term "shamanism" has expanded to encompass practitioners of a universal complex that is consistent through time and space. This broad use of the term is very controversial, as it is a term used by Western anthropologists to classify and study disparate groups of people. It is also used by Indigenous People themselves as a common and universal term across diverse cultures and languages, and in neoshamanism, which, at times, draws from various traditions.

Now the terms are used so generally, however, that one can become very confused! In some accounts, a shaman may be a particular type of medicine man.[134] In others, "medicine man" and "medicine woman" may be used because shamans no longer exist in a particular culture or because they do not admit to the role that now has such negative connotations. In still other accounts, shamans are equated with witches, healers, priests, and ritual specialists.

A shaman's role is not that of a specialist. Traditional and contemporary shamans are members of their family and community, and fill other roles such as hunter, farmer, or even banker, psychologist, and academic.

SEE ALSO: **ZOROASTRIANISM**

SHAMANISM

TERMS SUCH AS "core shamanism," "neoshamanism," and "real shamanism" are debated topics among scholars, the interested public, and shamans themselves. Held in Moscow in June 1999, a groundbreaking conference drew together shamans and researchers from a wide range of perspectives and disciplines at the leading edge of shamanic studies. Hosted by the Russian Academy of Sciences and sponsored by the Foundation for Shamanic Studies and others, the International Congress on Shamanism and Other Traditional Beliefs and Practices asked the question "What is shamanism anyway?"[135] Is it a religion? An archetypal complex of activities? A phenomenon of local cultures? Michael Harner called it a path of knowledge, not of faith; such knowledge is experiential, and to acquire it, one has to step through the shaman's doorway. The Siberian shamans at the conference—the "real shamans," as they came to be called—stressed that spirit work is serious business, potentially very dangerous for the uninitiated. It should not be undertaken without proper protection, training, guidance, and knowledge, which includes understanding of protocols.

Joan Townsend (professor emeritus, University of Manitoba) suggested that we need consensus about terminology and offered a working definition of shamanism and five essential criteria: direct contact and communication with spirits, control of spirits, control of shamanic states of consciousness, soul flight, and a focus on this material world. She pointed out how shamans work on behalf of their community to deal with the everyday problems of this world. Neoshamanism, on the other hand, is about individual discovery and self-awareness; the two should not be confused.

Such a definition distinguishes shamans from other practitioners such as channelers and psychics. At the same time, definitions of shamanism are evolving, as is shamanism itself.

SEE ALSO: **HARNER, MICHAEL**

SHAMANISM—DEFINITION AND MEANING

JUHA PENTIKÄINEN ATTRIBUTES the concept of shamanism to the Tungus word "saman," which came from Russian literature to its Western use at the end of the 1600s.[136] Shamanism is defined not as a religion but as a "worldview system" or a "grammar of mind" and by Michael Harner as a way of life.

Today, it is generally accepted in the current literature that shamanism is a universal complex with the particular defining characteristic of the shamanic journey. At the same time, the universality of core shamanism has adapted to local ecologies and histories. There is much controversy, however, that still pits one school of thought and one scholar against another.

Mircea Eliade, for example, defines shamanism as one of the archaic techniques of ecstasy. But equation of shamanism with the ecstatic state or trance as a universal is controversial. Scholars such as Juha Pentikäinen (drawing on the writings of Åke Hultkrantz) sees Eliade's meaning as so broad that it includes, at times, the spirit possession cults of medicine men in northern and eastern Africa, which other scholars think do not belong under the umbrella of shamanism.[137]

It is important to recognize, however, that while most scholars see Siberia as the "cradle" of shamanism and the origin of the term, "shamanism" has become the general and broad term for a cross-cultural complex that can now encompass specific terms for "shaman" in native languages throughout the world, as well as new expressions of classic practices. It is also important to note that Western anthropologists did much to popularize the term. It was used in order to name people, practices, and objects of study. The term "shamanism" became a way to categorize and know the "Other."

SEE ALSO: **NEOSHAMANISM AND NEOSHAMANS**

SHAMANISM AND ALTERNATIVE MEDICINE

"ALTERNATIVE MEDICINE," "Holistic medicine," and "complementary medicine" are terms used today to describe healing modalities that do not fit under the umbrella of mainstream, allopathic Western medicine and may include Chinese medicine, acupuncture, and ortho-molecular medicine. Many scholars worldwide have contributed to the shamanic revival and advocate for shamanic healing as a legitimate form of alternative medicine and holistic healing. And therapists in many modalities draw on shamanism and other Indigenous healing methods as transformative techniques for finding wholeness. They may practice shamanism themselves or work collaboratively with shamans in clinics or other settings. And in many contexts, traditional shamans or those newly discovering their shamanic ancestry are training as psychologists and psychotherapists.

Mention is made here of a few of the many scholars and alternative health practitioners interested in shamanism and its applications today. Sandra Ingerman has written about soul retrieval.[138] Stanley Krippner has written extensively on dreamwork, on the "inner shaman," and on his experiments in telepathy and shamanism, among other phenomena that cannot be explained by conventional science or medicine.

Stanislav Grof coined the term "holotropic breathwork" and developed the technique to induce "wholeness" in consciousness.[139] Breathwork has developed into what practitioners are calling "shamanic breathwork."

Very notably, Carl Jung drew inspiration from both Joseph Campbell and Mircea Eliade, incorporating various shamanic techniques such as mandalas and dreamwork into his psychotherapeutic practice.

Bradford Keeney co-founded the Keeney Institute for Healing, which is dedicated to the development and dissemination of spirituality and ecstatic healing. He suggests that healing is about being "shaken up" so you let go of whatever the mind is stuck in, thereby achieving an empty mind.[140] Trauma releasing exercises (TRE) are surely an extension of the "shaking medicine" of the Kalahari Bushmen on which Keeney's healing practice is based.

Eye movement desensitization and reprocessing (EMDR), which uses bilateral sensory input such as hand tapping or side-to-side eye movements to relieve stress, must have its origins in the shamanic view of balance as essential to health and wellness.

The Foundation for Shamanic Studies, founded by Michael Harner, supports practitioners to combine shamanic techniques with their alternative healing modality and supports traditional shamans to expand their geographic area to the international.

The Ringing Rocks Foundation, which produced the *Profiles of Healing* series, describes ecstatic healing practices on four continents as an alternative to mainstream medicine.

The entire field of spiritual ecology and the back-to-nature movement urge people to learn from the wilderness. Shamanic healing provides an answer to humanity's troubles. As an Iglulik shaman of the Canadian Arctic told Danish traveler Knud Rasmussen in the 1920s, "The only true wisdom lives far from mankind, out in the great loneliness, and it can be reached only through suffering. Privation and suffering alone can open the mind of man to all that is hidden to others."

SEE ALSO: **REVIVAL OF SHAMANISM**

SHAMANIC CULTURES, SHAMANIC TRADITIONS, SHAMANIC KNOWLEDGE

SHAMANIC, SHAMANIST, OR shamanistic (all terms used interchangeably in the literature) cultures have persisted into the present day even in areas where there are no practicing shamans. Political and religious suppression has forced many ideas into the background or made people afraid to acknowledge their traditions.

It is important to distinguish between two types of shamanic knowledge: that owned collectively by all or most members of a culture and that which is the prerogative of the shaman or shamans within that tradition. Members of a culture will share core beliefs and practices and may have spirit helpers, amulets, and so on, but a shaman's paraphernalia will be unique and proprietary.

SHAMANIC CRISIS

IF A PERSON becomes very ill and doesn't recover or experiences extreme trouble or loss, they may be diagnosed by another shaman or by the spirits as undergoing a shamanic illness or crisis. Not all potential shamans want to accept the role. It is a great responsibility and can be dangerous, but if they refuse it, the spirits may let them know they will become sick again.

The crisis may be induced as part of a shamanic initiation. The initiate may be killed and then resuscitated by a divine being or monster, as among some Australian Aborigines.[141] In other cases, spiritual dismemberment may take place after which the person becomes reconstituted as a shaman. Or the person may undergo a shamanic death and resurrection to be reborn as a shaman. While outsiders may see such experiences as merely symbolic or imaginary, we should remember that Western allopathic medicine has documented the resuscitation of patients whose hearts stopped beating and who were deemed clinically dead.

The shamanic role, writes Joseph Campbell, results from "intercourse with envisioned spirits; this intercourse having been established, usually in early adolescence, by way of a severe psychological breakdown of the greatest stress and even danger to life. The extraordinary uniformity in far-separated parts of the earth of the images and stages of this 'shamanic crisis' suggests that they may represent the archetypes of a psychological exaltation, related on one hand to schizophrenia and on the other to the ecstasies of the yogis, saints, and dervishes of the high religions."[142]

SHAMANHOOD

THE TERM "SHAMANHOOD" is used in the ethnographic literature to describe the act of being a shaman; the assumption of the shaman's role; or the nature, condition, or state of being a shaman.

SHAMAN'S TOOLKIT

A SHAMAN'S TOOLKIT consists of objects, materials, techniques, and esoterica used in shamanizing and will be specific to a particular shaman.[143] It may be constructed by shamans themselves or be a collective effort of their family or broader community. In the Darhad Valley in Mongolia, for example, there are specialists in drum making, while a group of women may be involved in making the shaman's dress. In some traditions, it will be expensive for a family or community to pay for everything a new shaman will need. Other things come directly to the shaman—things seen in a dream or on a journey that then appear in physical form and become amulets or talismans to be kept in the shaman's medicine bag. The Darhad shaman Maamaa, for example, has a large bag of crystals collected from his sacred mountain that he uses in healing. Such items are "power"; they are alive and sentient. Sometimes items may be passed down through the family line. Ancestors and other spirit helpers also form part of the toolkit.

The term is also used to include the forces that the shaman may call upon—"the sun, moon, stars, mountains, rivers, rocks, trees, thunder, the echo, the rainbow, homes, fields, recompense or karma, beds, marriage, swords, the harvest, the year, the *liu sheng* [a musical instrument], ceremonial drum, and even the sound of the ceremonial drum are considered to be living things."[144]

SHAMAN'S ROLE

THERE IS CONSISTENCY to the role of a shaman worldwide at the same time as there is great diversity among shamanist cultures and even among practitioners in any one tradition. Any group may have one or more shamans, each with their own area of expertise. An often-misunderstood role, especially in neoshamanism, is the shaman as protector of their immediate circle against outsiders. And shamans may do battle to see who has the strongest spirits, or there may be battles between healing shamans and sorcerers.

A core shamanic principle is the interdependence of shaman and spirit: A shaman requires spirit help do their work, while the spirit world needs the shaman to influence this world. But particulars depend on a shaman's helping spirits and differ according to the context—urban or rural, hunters or farmers, and so on. In a hunting culture, for example, shamans may determine the movements of game. For farmers, shamans may be needed to call in the rain or send it away. Such differences will be evident in a shaman's toolkit. It is never a specialist role, however, as shamans are also members of their society. In the past, they would take on the roles of their culture—hunter, herder, wife, father, and so on—while today, shamans may be bankers, psychologists, artists, or even anthropologists.

Some shamans do not want to accept the role, saying it is too much responsibility or too dangerous. Pablo Amaringo, an ayahuasca shaman of the Peruvian Amazon, gave up taking ayahuasca and practicing shamanism because of several fights he had with other practitioners of magic, including a sorcerer. At first, he was angry with his spirits for not protecting him, but his spirits told him it was his mission to talk about the spirit world in the difficult time that humanity is going through via his paintings.

A shaman may influence the weather, appease the spirits when a societal norm has been breached, locate lost objects, conduct rituals and ceremonies, divine, interpret dreams, accompany the spirits of the dead to the other world, heal sickness or sometimes cause it, perform extractions, foretell the future, converse with the dead, and retrieve lost souls, among many other activities.

Knud Rasmussen writes about the role of Padlermiut shamans of Hudson Bay before the 1930s:

 As has already been observed, angatkut are first and foremost healers, but they can also examine a road that is to be traveled; in that case, however, they must seek solitude far away from people. There they sit down at a place where there are no footprints, draw their hood up over their head and the hands right inside the armholes; they close their eyes, and then try to see the road that is to be examined. Sometimes they fall asleep and see their visions in a dream, or a spirit comes down invisibly from the air, hovers over them, speaks from the air and tells them what the road is like. If there are lurking dangers, these must be avoided by the traveler seeking other roads, and, if the advice of the shaman is not taken, one becomes ill."[145]

SEE ALSO: **EXTRACTION, EXORCISM; PSYCHOPOMP; RITUAL AND CEREMONY**

SHAMAN'S HELPER

IN SOME TRADITIONS and some contexts, a shaman may have a helper or assistant, sometimes a shaman-in-training. In preparing for the shaman's ritual, a helper might collect and prepare plants if the shaman uses them, lay and "feed" the fire, assist the shaman to dress, and take care that no one comes too close to the shaman or their equipment.

While the shaman is in an altered state of consciousness, the helper may continue drumming for the shaman or check to see that they don't come into danger by getting too close to the fire or falling over an obstacle.

SHAPESHIFTING

IN SHAMANISM, "SHAPESHIFTING" refers to the ability of an animal or human to metamorphose into another form. This may happen for any number of reasons—to acquire one another's capabilities, for protection, and so on. In a painting of an ayahuasca vision, a group of people are peacefully taking ayahuasca while a sorcerer tries to cause them harm.[146] They transform themselves into wolves to hide from the sorcerer.

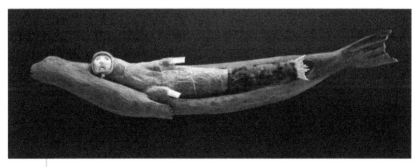

A shaman shapeshifting into a seal. Museum Purchase, Rasmuson Foundation Art Acquisition Fund, Anchorage Museum, 2010.

SEE ALSO: **MERGING; SORCERY**

SHINTO IS A Japanese shamanist tradition that blends Indigenous Ainu and ancestral Japanese spirituality. Shinto, meaning "way of gods," is based in living in harmony with nature and with the spirits that reside in nature in trees, rivers, mountains, and so on. As these spirits were honored, shrines developed. At such places, deities and the spirits of ancestors could be met and asked for protection, prayed to for benefits, or asked for a good harvest.

At one time, there were about 190,000 Shinto shrines in Japan. With the arrival of Buddhism, however, the number was drastically reduced to about 80,000 today.[147] Initially, Shinto deities were intangible and invisible but later were represented as figures because Buddhist deities were given form in statues.[148]

Today, according to some sources, fewer and fewer Japanese are exclusively Shinto but instead visit both Buddhist temples and Shinto shrines; however, Shinto practices seem to be embedded in Japanese life even if they are not recognized as such. The Japanese term *shinrin-yoku*, meaning "forest bathing" or "taking in the forest atmosphere," has become a fundamental element in alternative medicine and preventive health care in Japan today and surely is rooted in Shinto and shamanism. Forest bathing has even been exported to the West, where it blends with Indigenous Peoples' ideas about well-being.

SIBERIA

SIBERIA IS A vast area, the largest region of the world's largest nation, extending over the Arctic and Subarctic regions of tundra, taiga, and grassland. As it is ecologically diverse, it is also diverse linguistically and culturally, more so than any other northern region.

Indigenous Peoples—Buryat Mongols, Yakuts, Tatars, Evens, Samoyeds, Tunguses, Chukchis, Yupiks, and others—are minority peoples in numbers and also in terms of their relationship with the Russian state and the dominant Russian culture and ideology.[149]

Indigenous Peoples of Siberia are struggling to maintain their identities and also to redefine them in post-Communist times. Under Russian rule for about 350 years, Russia's ethnic minorities were affected by eastward expansion, colonization, and pacification under the Imperial Russian Empire, as well as by decimation by disease and massacre. Forcible conversion to Christianity began in the 18th century. Especially after the 1930s, minorities were affected by administrative pressures during the period of the Soviet Union and by the assimilationist policies of the Communist Party. Educational reforms initiated by Nikita Khrushchev in the 1950s eliminated many languages, while the boarding school system removed children from their communities. Khrushchev's initiation of a "Conquest of Siberia" program was carried on by Leonid Brezhnev with devastating ecological and demographic consequences. Today, as with Indigenous Peoples elsewhere, Siberian languages and cultural traditions are at risk. Collectivization and settlement policies have altered their traditional nomadism such that one-third of the Indigenous population is now fully urbanized. Economic alternatives have not been provided to the traditional means of subsistence—cattle ranching, horse breeding and reindeer husbandry, hunting and fishing, trapping and gathering. Russia's largest scientific organization, the Russian Academy of Sciences Siberian Division, established the Institute of the Northern Minorities Problems in 1991 to address ongoing difficulties of state–Indigenous Peoples relations.

As with other Indigenous Peoples of the circumpolar world, Siberian Native Peoples are shamanist by tradition. Shamans suffered severe persecution, especially under Joseph Stalin, including death or incarceration in concentration camps. Communist propaganda, which outlawed shamans as "parasites," was intended to create fear and distrust in their communities. Shamans' drums were burned as symbols of shamans' power, and paraphernalia were confiscated for museum collections.[150] Even today, some Siberians will not mention the word "shaman" out of respect for their remembered power and also in recognition of the success of the Soviet propaganda in undermining the traditional belief system. Many Siberians still live with the persecution and loss of family members who were shamans.[151]

In the past, each unit, village, or clan had a shaman, but in 1997, according to one anthropologist, few practicing shamans remained: Most Sakhas, for instance, considered only five to be genuine, and even their authenticity was contested.[152] At the same time, their legitimacy is being reinstated through Russian and international efforts and support. Shamans at a 1984 conference were told they "no longer had occasion to feel shame, as shamanism had ceased to be an object of opprobrium—that it was, instead, an integral part of identity-building national self-awareness."[153]

Contemporary writers describe shamanism as the religion of most Siberians;[154] as an ethnic religion and culture;[155] as a way of life;[156] and as the pivot of native Siberian society[157] in which the chosen leader, or shaman, occupies a central role but that permeates a culture and survives the deaths of shamans.[158] The shamanic worldview of Indigenous cultures remains distinctive from state ideology and culture in Russia today. Siberian Native Peoples define their future in terms of their traditions, which are symbols of survival and strength: "We have survived both communism and capitalism," an elder remarked at the 2000 conference in Yakutsk City on shamanism.[159] The ancestral tradition of shamanism is now the focus around which ethnic identities are coalescing at the local, regional, national, and international levels.

Siberia is considered by many, if not most, scholars of shamanism to be the "classic" form of shamanism, with a vast ethnographic literature in Russian, English, and other languages that discusses and documents it as the homeland of the circumpolar shamanic complex. In Siberia today, some shamans continue their ancestral shamanic lineage; others are being initiated as neoshamans.[160] And while in the past, shamans worked for their local group, today Siberian shamans participate in international events, teach in their own schools, and travel widely to teach and shamanize. An extraordinary revival is taking place, supported by the combined efforts of Russian and international scholars, the Russian Academy of Sciences, the Foundation of Shamanic Studies, and the International Society for Academic Research on Shamanism (ISARS), along with many other individuals and organizations.

SEE ALSO: **CIRCUMPOLAR SHAMANISM**

THE SKELETON MOTIF is found in humanity's oldest art and artifacts, including the rock art of India, Australia, Norway, and many other places. And it continues to be a common motif today in the expressive arts from dance to painting in many cultures. It represents the ability to see the essence of an animal or person, which is sometimes referred to as "X-ray vision."

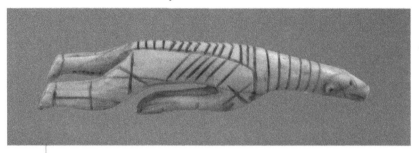

The Dorset way of life developed in the Canadian Arctic by about 500 BCE and then vanished from the archaeological record between 1200 and 1500 CE. Archaeological excavations of Dorset sites have produced many carvings in wood and ivory, including hundreds of polar bears. This is one of the most fascinating. When I first studied it in the collections of the Canadian Museum of History, I saw it as a swimming or flying bear and as having a shamanic purpose because of its extended neck. The inscribed lines mark joints in places— Inuit today say joints are places of power where Spirit resides. And with the skeletal motif, perhaps the carver was connecting with the essence of the polar bear as the most powerful spirit animal or jour- neying to the spirit world in the form of a bear. Igloolik area. Carving, Middle Dorset, A.D. 500–1200. Canadian Museum of History, nhHd-1: 2655, IMG2008-0215-011-Dm.

Skeletons and skulls are motifs in the ayahuasca visions of Pablo Amaringo.[161] The skeleton dance of Tibetan Buddhism, in which the performer dresses as a skeleton, represents one of its basic teachings: the imper- manence of life. The skeleton communicates the essential truth about life—ultimate disintegration of all worldly phenomena including the body as well as our states of mind.[162] And everywhere, bones of animal spirit helpers

are kept as amulets or carved into effigies for the power
they bestow on the bearer.

SEE ALSO: **X-RAY VISION**

SMOKE, INCENSE, SMUDGE

A VARIETY OF plants are burned in shamanic cultures.
Plants that produce a pleasing scent when burned are said
to please the spirits, while the smoke of sacred plants can
permeate the thin membrane that separates the worlds.

The burning of plants for sacred purposes seems to
be almost universal, whether to appease and beguile the
spirits, open the way to the other world, expel negative
forces, or cleanse and purify a space or participants in a
ceremony. In some contexts, the smoke may be inhaled
as medicine. Plants may be used in loose, powdered form
or as whole branches or combined into incense cones
or sticks.

The Hmong of Southeast Asia use sacred elephant
grass in an annual clan-based ceremony to chase away
all bad things from one's body and protect the body for
another year. The grass is passed over the body of every
member of the clan, or it is held up or placed at the top
of a small tree for each member to walk under.[163] The
Tsaatan of northern Mongolia lay a branch of native cedar
to smolder on top of their central stove; the smoke then
travels up to the opening at the top of their tents to reach
the spirits. Plants gathered from the higher reaches of the
mountains where the Tsaatan live are said to be the most
powerful because the human aura is least.

First Nations and Métis of Canada burn primarily
sweet grass, cedar, juniper, or tobacco, and the Artemisias
or wild sages as smudge in a clam or abalone shell, stone,
or other container. A feather is used to fan the embers
and spread the smoke. Copal, a tree resin, is burned in

Mexico. In Tibet, plant material is combined with other materials such as minerals, metals, and tree barks to make a composite medicinal incense. The therapeutic effects depend on the altitude at which the plants were picked, time of year they were gathered, color, degree of maturity of the plant, and exposure to the wind, sun, and other elements, among other factors.

Whether used by a shaman or other individual, protocols are followed in gathering the plants, in plant preparation, and in disposing of the ash.

Incense for sale at Mörön Market, Mongolia, 2007.

SONG, POWER

ANYONE MAY RECEIVE a song from the spirit world, which conveys power to call in and communicate with their spirit helpers. When singing a power song, one becomes power-filled and able to navigate the spirit world protected and guided. Shamans, who might have many power songs, may use theirs in a ritual context to administer the medicine of the song and heal their patients or protect them from supernatural attack. Power songs may come in a dream, on a shamanic journey, in a vision, or in meditation. They may be requested or just come spontaneously.

Numerous recordings have been made of shamans' songs, especially to do with the ayahuasca ceremony. Ayahuasca visions include seeing large groups of people who are singing, dancing, and playing instruments, while the ayahuasca spirits themselves often arrive singing.[164] Songs may belong to an individual or be meant to be sung in a group. They may be passed on orally, written down by the owners or an intermediary, or represented visually as among the Shipibo of Peru, where "the songs assume the form of a geometric pattern, a *quinquin* design which penetrates the patient's body and settles down permanently."[165]

Writing about his stay with the Copper Inuit of the Canadian Arctic, Diamond Jenness (1886–1969) observed that their singing was accompanied by a swaying from side to side while the feet remained in place. Note that Jenness writes, "A spirit is supposed to be speaking all through." Like many other writers on shamanism, past and present, Jenness does not believe what he is documenting.

From generation to generation, from inyuit sivulingni, 'men of the first times,' as the natives say, various incantations, akeutit, have been handed down to appease or drive away the malignant spirits. The incantation is usually sung by all the people, with one of their shamans standing in the centre of the ring; and as they sing their bodies sway from side to side, though their feet remain stationary. At the conclusion of the refrain the shaman invokes his familiars, and with their aid produces the desired result. Children are generally excluded from these performances. Many of the incantations are very old and have lost whatever meaning they had originally; but this does not lessen their potency. I heard one sung during a snow-storm in the late summer of 1915. Tusayok and Kesullik had no tent, so they improvised a rude shelter by stretching some skins between two crags; but since in spite of this they were very cold and uncomfortable, Tusayok chanted an incantation and repeated it over and over again for about an hour. There were only about half a dozen words in it, and each taken by itself was intelligible enough, but no one had any clear idea of what the whole song meant. Tusayok thought, however, that the mere singing of this incantation, even though he was not himself a shaman, might have the effect of driving away the evil shades or spirits who were causing the storm and produce fine weather again. Literally translated the song ran:

I come again, I, again.
I come again, I, again. Do you not know?
I come again, I, again."*

*A spirit is supposed to be speaking all through.

SEE ALSO: **AYAHUASCA**

SORCERY

THERE IS NO universally accepted definition of sorcery in anthropology, but it usually involves the intent to harm by manipulating supernatural forces. In the anthropological literature, a practitioner of sorcery, or sorcerer, may be called a medicine man or medicine woman or shaman sorcerer; the latter distinguishes a sorcerer from a healing shaman. Michael Harner, for example, describes the shaman of Carlos Castaneda's classic study *The Teachings of Don Juan: A Yaqui Way of Knowledge* as a sorcerer shaman who uses witchcraft and black magic against his enemies.[166]

SOUL

IN SHAMANISM, "SOUL" is often used interchangeably with "spirit" to mean the essence of someone.

SEE ALSO: **SPIRITS**

SOUL LOSS AND SOUL RETRIEVAL

SOUL RETRIEVAL IS a classic shamanic healing technique found cross-culturally, although its particulars depend on the cultural context and the shaman. At the core of shamanist cosmology is the idea that all illness, whether physical, spiritual, emotional, or mental, results from the loss of a person's spirit, soul, or soul part; the result of such loss will show as "disharmony" or "dispiritedness" in a person's life. A shaman journeys to the spirit world to locate and retrieve the lost soul and then restore it to the person's body, sometimes by using a soul catcher.

A soul or soul part may be stolen by a sorcerer or other person with evil intent. A person's soul or part of it may depart the body to protect itself under difficult circumstances such as an accident, an attack, a fright, abuse, or other trauma. A person may lose it or leave it behind in the other world if they are journeying without proper guidance or knowledge. Traditional shamans say that hallucinogens can make it easy to enter an altered state of consciousness, but without the proper guidance, participants may not return fully and will suffer from addictions, depression, or other afflictions.

When someone is missing a part of their essence and power, they are left vulnerable to bad entities entering to take its place.

The Hmong of northern Thailand perform a spirit-calling ceremony. Held on the last day of the Hmong year and just before the first day of the new year, its purpose is to recall souls if they have departed for some reason.

Eggs, one for each member of the family, are put into a bowl. An elder or shaman performs the ceremony to call back each member's soul into their egg. Afterward, the eggs are boiled and returned to each person, who will eat their egg, meaning their souls have returned to them.[167]

Today, soul retrieval is associated with practitioners such as Sandra Ingerman and Michael Harner.

SOUND

IN SHAMANIC TRADITIONS, thunder, the wind, bird-song ... are the voice of Spirit. Shamans communicate with Spirit through such sounds, sometimes expressing them in their power songs. Such sounds are also a sonic bridge to Spirit, while some people describe sounds as spirits themselves. As Tuvan shaman throat singer Nikolay Oorzhak expressed the connection, "A sound is a spirit that moves through space."

SOUND HEALING

"SOUND HEALING," ALSO referred to as "sound therapy" and, "vibrational medicine," is increasing in popularity as a modern-day healing modality and alternative to allopathic medicine. It incorporates the human voice, crystal bowls, gongs, tuning forks, chimes, and such to enable mental and physical relaxation and stimulate healing. Schools have developed along with certification programs to standardize its techniques and outcomes. Results may include a lower heart rate, reduced respiratory rate, reduced stress level, and calmed brain-wave patterns. Its effects are mental as well as physiological because the effects are felt, not just heard. Like many of today's healing modalities, it has archaic roots.

I met Bokova Evdokia Nikolaevna, an Even composer and scholar, when she gave a paper on Even folk musical instruments at a shamanism conference in Russia in 2000.[168] The paper was important because, she said, "few people now use the instruments of our nations and the new generation doesn't know them." The Even, a northern Siberian Indigenous People who still practice shamanism, are nomadic people who made their instruments from what they had—mammoth bone, reindeer horn, metal for mouth harps, other local materials for stringed harps and rattles. Very complicated instruments were made by masters. "We are the last to remember our songs and instruments," she said. "We decorate our clothing and we decorate our instruments. Every bell had its own sound and name; the beautiful sounds of each bell had a cleansing quality." Bokova described four types of instruments: stringed, percussive, membrane, and whistling. But her voice—she treats people with a voice much deeper than her spoken voice—is perhaps her most powerful healing instrument.

I had asked her for a healing song, but she refused because her voice was not good due to there being too much smoke in the room. The next day, however, she sang a song she had composed for me to wish me, and all the audience, good health. She can treat with her voice, and she can treat with her eyes. "Be happy," she said to me toward the end. "I convey good thoughts, feelings to you through my voice to bring you health." The Russian conference organizer described how Bokova had brought everyone together, drawn good feelings out of the group, and focused them in her song.

I felt the effects in my upper body, across my chest, and was told by others that a feeling of warmth across the chest and heart area shows the skill of the singer. I realized that when such people are singing traditional songs, they are not just relaying events but are keeping alive the feelings and experiences generated by the events, bringing past time into the present.

SEE ALSO: **MOUTH HARP, JEW'S HARP, JAW'S HARP**

SPECIALIZATION

TRADITIONALLY, ALMOST EVERY family, group, or community would have a shaman and sometimes more than one. Shamans developed areas of experience depending on their own abilities and on those of their spirit helpers, including ancestors. People would go to whichever shaman was known to be most helpful for a particular problem. If a shaman was not successful in, for example, changing the weather or identifying good hunting, then people would go to someone else! In this way, shamans were "made" by their clients, and clients were healed by the shamans in whom they put their trust.

Today, when so many shamans have disappeared or no longer practice, shamans work across traditional cultural boundaries, including healing outsiders from very different cultural backgrounds. I was once told by a Hmong woman shaman in northern Thailand that she couldn't treat me if I were a practicing Christian because our spirits would be in conflict. Some issues could be handled only by the "big" shamans; such a shaman could kill someone if they had to, if a member of their family were being threatened, for example, but then that shaman would themselves die. Generally, shamans practice either "good" or "bad" medicine—healing or harming. This book is primarily concerned with the former.

SHAMANS WORK IN partnership with their helping spirits, also called familiar spirits or familiars, spirit helpers, guardian spirits, or allies. These protect them in both Ordinary and Non-Ordinary Realities. Helping spirits might be in the form of a human, often an ancestor, an animal, or even a plant. In some cases, the elements—earth, air, fire, water—might be called upon for help.

Knud Rasmussen transcribed the words of a Padlermiut, or Caribou Inuit, shaman of the Canadian Arctic describing his initiation as a shaman and his acquisition of his helping spirit.

 As soon as I had become alone, Perqanaq [my instructor was my wife's father, Perqanaq] enjoined me to think of one single thing all the time I was to be there, to want only one single thing, and that was to draw Pinga's attention to the fact that there I sat and wished to be a shaman ... Pinga should own me. My novitiate took place in the middle of the coldest winter, and I, who never got anything to warm me, and must not move, was very cold, and it was so tiring having to sit without daring to lie down, that sometimes it was as if I died a little. Only towards the end of the thirty days did a helping spirit come to me, a lovely and beautiful helping spirit, whom I had never thought of; it was a white woman; she came to me whilst I had collapsed, exhausted, and was sleeping. But still I saw her life-like, hovering over me, and from that day I could not close my eyes or dream without seeing her. There is this remarkable thing about my helping spirit, that I have never seen her while awake, but only in dreams. She came to me from Pinga and was a sign that Pinga had now noticed me and would give me powers that would make me a shaman. I had become the shaman of my village, and it did happen that my neighbours or people from a long distance away called me to heal a sick person, or to 'inspect a course' if they were going to travel."[169]

As there is both good and evil in this physical world, so is there good and evil in the unseen worlds; both are inhabited by helpful as well as harmful entities. When on a journey, a shaman must be able to face many challenges and overcome many obstacles. They may be seeking to remove evil spirits or unwanted influences from a client or from a place or object and may have to battle bad spirits encountered on their journey. The Tsaatan shaman Anai[170] spoke about how she was treating a patient but the evil spirit in the patient jumped into her instead, causing her severe problems.

Shamans are as powerful as their helping spirits and must also be strong enough to manage their spirits. Classic stories tell of shamans battling one another and their spirits or battling Buddhist lamas, and of sorcerer shamans whose intent is to harm others or better themselves at another's expense. In some traditions, shamans are specific to a family or clan and act against a competing group; their spirits would protect their group's interests. Some spirits, such as the Nganasan idol, are what Michael Harner has called "ethnocentric compassionate spirits." This idol helped the Nganasan of northern Siberia defend themselves against the Nenets when the Nenets tried to enter their territory in the 18th century. As the helping spirit of a famous warrior at the time, it was a family, lineage, or clan spirit that was then passed on to a shaman in Soviet times. After the shaman died, the idol is said to have brought very bad luck— death or illness—to those who ended up with it, the last one being Harner, who decided to break the pattern by returning it to its homeland on the Taimyr Peninsula in Siberia.[171]

The ill fortune conveyed by the Nganasan idol on outsiders underscores how shamanic objects themselves are "enspirited" and filled with power. One should avoid even touching a shaman's belongings, since the spirits that protect a shaman and reside in their paraphernalia can be dangerous to others.

SEE ALSO: **EXTRACTION, EXORCISM; JOURNEY, SHAMANIC**

SUCKING TUBE, SOUL CATCHER

IN MANY PARTS of the world, a common method of curing was extraction of pain or injury by sucking malevolent spirits from a patient's body via the use of a hollowed-out sucking tube or sometimes by using the mouth. One end of the tube was placed on the patient's body while the shaman then sucked the unwanted influence out, appearing to swallow it or breathe it in and then regurgitate, spit, or breathe it out. Sucking tubes might also be called soul catchers.

Among the Tillamook of the U.S. Pacific coast, only female shamans sucked to cure (while male shamans used the drawing-with-the-hands method of healing). Some sucked out blood, others a white or black substance, although they sucked with their lips rather than with a tube and then "spit the substance in a bucket of water or spread it on the hot ashes of a fire. If it was a severe illness, she might both drown and burn it."[172]

The film *Pomo Shaman* contains footage of Essie Parrish, who allowed her sucking ceremony to be filmed in 1963. What follows is a description from the American Indian Film Gallery, talking both about the ceremony and recognizing intellectual property rights of traditional practices, as permission was granted to document the ceremony and also to distribute the film.

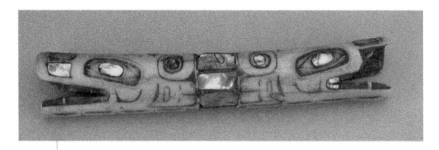

This cast of a shaman's sucking tube was made by people of the Dorset culture and dates to about 1000 CE. The Dorset people descended from immigrants from Siberia, the first occupants of Arctic North America who inhabited what is now Arctic Canada for more than 3,000 years. Their disappearance about 500 years ago is attributed to invasion by the modern-day Inuit. Soulcatcher, Thimshian, 1905 or earlier. Canadian Museum of History, VII-C-160.

 The film *Pomo Shaman* documents the second and final night of a Kashaya Pomo healing ceremony led by Essie Parrish (1903–1979), a spiritual, cultural and political head of the Kashaya Pomo community and one of the only southwestern Pomo sucking doctors who still practiced this ancient form of doctoring. Along with her good friend, Cache Creek Pomo medicine woman and fellow basket weaver Mabel McKay, Parrish would be the last of the sucking doctors in California—and probably the last in the entire country.

"The ceremony took place June 1, 1963, in a ceremonial roundhouse of the Southwestern Pomo (now more commonly referred to as Kashaya or Kashaya Pomo) near Stewarts Point, California. During the ceremony (which is presented without narration), Parrish enters a trance and cures a patient with the aid of a spiritual instrument used to suck out the patient's illness. Parrish only gave the film crew one chance to shoot the ceremony, with no equipment allowed inside the roundhouse where the ceremony took place. All cameras and lighting were setup to shoot through knot holes in the walls, which explains the films dark, high- contrast appearance.

"William Heick made *Pomo Shaman* while Director and Chief Cinematographer for the University of California at Berkeley's National Science Foundation supported the American Indian Film Project. It is an edited version of Heick's larger work *Sucking Doctor* (1963, 45 minutes). Heick's *Pomo Shaman* grants us a rare chance to experience a ceremony generally off-limits to cameras. According to Essie's son, Parrish only agreed to be filmed knowing that their traditions were going to be preserved on film for both their community as well as the outside world. To this day, the Kashaya watch this film before performing healing ceremonies since the film, according to Essie's son, is 'infused with her healing powers.'

"CFA is aware of the sensitivity in presenting indigenous cultural heritage and have sought permission from the Kashaya Pomo of Northern California, or more specifically Essie's son Otis Parrish, to present this film. He has given us their blessing, as well as a warning that our audiences may feel signs of his mother's healing powers and begin to 'heal for ourselves individually.'"[173]

SWEAT LODGE

SWEAT LODGES, SOMETIMES called simply "sweats," are for cleansing and purification in a ceremonial context and are found in many parts of the world. They may be simple structures of tree limbs and hides or more permanent structures for regular use. A sweat may be part of a shamanic initiation or used to cleanse participants physically and spiritually under the guidance of a shaman or other practitioner. In some traditions, only the men would sweat, but today it is not unusual for women to be included in these ceremonies. Steam is produced by pouring water on a central fire pit made of stones. The photos show two types of Native American sweat lodges.

Nez Percé sweat lodge.
Photograph by Edward S. Curtis, 1910.

Hupa sweat house. This sweat lodge is built underground and covered with a wood plank roof; it is surrounded by a wall of large rocks. Photograph by Edward S. Curtis, 1923.

SYNCRETISM

"SYNCRETISM" IS DEFINED as the blending or amalgamation of cultures, religions, philosophies, beliefs, or practices.

It is used here to refer to the assimilation of shamanic beliefs and practices into the dominant religions such as Christianity, Islam, Buddhism, and Judaism. Whether these ideas are acceptable to scholars and practitioners in those religions is controversial. Sometimes, the practice will be similar, but the terms used will differ; for example, "exorcism" is used in Christianity—the shamanic equivalent is "extraction." Syncretism is also apparent in the fields of holistic and alternative healing, psychology, and psychotherapy, which have adopted and reframed many shamanic techniques. Energy work, a broadly encompassing field of alternative medicine, refers to "good" and "bad" or "positive" and "negative" energies, as shamanism refers to "good" and "bad" spirits.

SEE ALSO: **BUDDHISM; CHRISTIANITY; ISLAM; JUDAISM**

TALISMAN

THE TRADITIONAL MEANING of "talisman" is an object that repels evil or harmful forces or energies away from or brings good luck to the holder. It might even refer to a person whose presence awards good luck to a situation such as a hunting party or sports event. Talisman is often used interchangeably and sometimes indiscriminately with the terms "charm," "fetish," and "amulet."

SEE ALSO: **AMULET; FETISH**

TANTRA

TANTRA IS AN esoteric practice generally associated with Buddhism and Hinduism. But as with so many other terms in this book, defining it is problematic. Tantric traditions are very diverse, and there are many conflicting ideas about their meaning and origins.[174] Like neoshamanism, neotantra has become popular in the West, but its roots and practices are misunderstood in the literature that sensationalizes it. The authors of *Shamanism and Tantra in the Himalayas* treat Tantra "essentially as a magical technique that exerts an influence on the world of polarities."[175] This is a very general definition, but their basic premise is relevant here in that Buddhism, Hinduism, and Nepali culture have all borrowed from shamanism. Although shamanic techniques have disappeared or gone underground in many parts of the world, in the Himalayan kingdom of Nepal, both shamanic and tantric techniques remain in full practice, the only culture in the world where this is so.[176]

"Demons" in Nepali shamanism are called "bad" or "evil" spirits elsewhere. Nepali shamans use psycho-active plants in their ceremonies, including the mythical "soma," which the authors show is made up of a blend of consciousness-altering plants, and they make pilgrimages to their sacred mountains, as shamanists do elsewhere. On the tantric side, thangka painting, which is ordinarily associated with Buddhism, has shamanic roots, and the sacred objects of Tantra include feathers, the drum, magical daggers, amulets, and journeying to the other world in an altered state of consciousness, among other classic elements. As well, Tantra is based in the tripartite shamanist cosmology and the four directions. While in

Hinduism practitioners invoke Ganesha, the elephant god, as the remover of obstacles before beginning any venture, all Nepali shamans invoke Ganesha as the first shaman in history and the guardian of the threshold.[177]

TIBETAN BÖN OR BON

WITH THE INVASION of Tibet by China in 1950, Tibetans fled to seek sanctuary in Nepal, Bhutan, and India. In India, Bonpos (followers of Bön) were able to establish the Tibetan Bonpo Foundation in 1967. Menri Monastery (Medicine Hill) was completed in northern India in 1978.

The Bön tradition of Tibet, now in practiced exile in northern India, is a syncretic blend of shamanism and Buddhism, predating Buddhism as a monastic system by about 1,800 years. It is unusual among shamanist traditions because of its transmission of knowledge via written text.

In Bön, there is an interplay between the shamanic and clerical aspects of Buddhism, producing what is called "shamanic Buddhism," the sophisticated body of shamanic practices within Tibetan Buddhism that "probably constitutes Tibet's most important single contribution to humanity."[178] Bön thus combines pursuit of enlightenment by a minority with concern for the well-being of all, including the lay majority, through sha-manic means such as accessing non-ordinary states of consciousness; maintaining good fortune, good luck, and a good relationship with the local gods; and protecting the household.[179] The lama, who develops power from long periods of retreat, is the key figure in Bön.

SEE ALSO: **SACRED GEOMETRY**

TIME AND SPACE

IN THE SHAMANIC cosmos, time and space operate differently from the linear time and defined, geographic space of the modern world. Time in Indigenous and traditional cultures is cyclical, based on the cycle of death and renewal of the natural world. And geography includes the layout of the Upper and Lower Worlds as part of the tripartite universe. Thus, shamans are able to travel backward or forward in time and to navigate the vastness of the shamanic cosmos. They can then intervene in events that alter the present, and thus future, circumstances of a client. For someone who is suffering from a sorcerer's attack, for example, a shaman may travel back in time or space to when and where the attack occurred and intervene to change the outcome.

TRANCE

THE TERM IS commonly used in the ethnographic literature to denote the altered state of consciousness a shaman enters when journeying. Some scholars say it doesn't apply to shamanism but is associated with practitioners such as mediums or hypnotists. To the layperson, it suggests a "half-consciousness" state, as suggested by its dictionary synonyms of "daze" or "stupor" that mislead about the shaman's purposeful state of awareness. The word is used occasionally in this book because a source uses it and because we lack a commonly accepted vocabulary in English for the shamanic experience.

TREE

THE COSMIC TREE, World Tree, or Tree of Life is a central image in shamanism, sometimes equated with the axis mundi. It constitutes, in physical form, the three worlds of the tripartite universe. The branches are the Upper World, the trunk is the Middle World, and the roots are the Lower World. Trees are entry points for shamans to enter the other worlds: By climbing a tree, the shaman ascends to the heavens or Sky World; by journeying into the roots of the tree, a shaman descends into the Lower World. It is common to find images of birds atop a tree (or a pole, which is a tree stripped of its branches), which represent the shaman's soul in flight ascending to the heavens.

SEE ALSO: **AXIS MUNDI; MIDDLE WORLD; UNDERWORLD OR LOWER WORLD; UPPER WORLD**

TRICKSTER

THE TRICKSTER ARCHETYPE is a universal, but its form will vary cross-culturally. Depending on the cultural context, a trickster may be clever or foolish but will play tricks on humans, breaking rules and otherwise disrupting conventions using unorthodox techniques. A trickster may be a person, god, or animal and may also be a shapeshifter. Coyote and Raven are common tricksters in Native American and First Nations traditions. Both feature in creation stories. Raven, for example, is celebrated on the Northwest Coast for stealing fire from the gods, whereas Coyote taught humans how to catch salmon.

Kokopelli, the hunchbacked flute player of the American Southwest, is a well-known figure in ancient rock art and among artists and artisans of the Navahos, Apaches, and others today. To some, he is a benevolent god; to others, he is a nuisance and a trickster.

SEE ALSO: **SHAPESHIFTING**

KNOWN AS *TSAATAN* (the Russian word for reindeer
herder) in Mongolia and *Dukha* in the anthropological literature,[181] the reindeer herders are Tuvan by ancestry but
were isolated from their relatives in Tuva upon closure of
the Russia–Mongolia border after 1991. Sometimes they
refer to themselves as Tuvan. They herd reindeer in the
higher reaches of the mountains of northern Mongolia,
whereas Darhad Mongolians graze yaks, goats, and sheep
on the grasslands of the lower altitudes. The Tsaatan and
Darhad Mongolians have coexisted and in some ways
blended, thus giving this area a different ethnic and
historical character from the predominant "Mongolian"
culture that has been heavily influenced by Buddhism.
Both groups retain a shamanic worldview that embodies
core elements of shamanism. But Tsaatan shamanism is
said, even by the Darhad, to be the strongest and most
authentic because it is closest to nature.

All Tsaatan have individual helping spirits that must
be honored and treated with respect; in return, these
spirits take care of them and the land on which they
depend. Some have very strong helping spirits as well as
the shaman's gift to navigate the spirit world on behalf
of their community. Each shaman is known for particular
strengths depending on their personalities and on the
characteristics of their spirit helpers and ancestors. The
shaman Suyan, who died some years ago at more than
100 years of age, was known for her reindeer medicine.
She would designate a spirit reindeer, marked by a red
string or ribbon, to protect and care for the herd. And she
made spirit bags for each person in the household as protection from sickness and bad things as well as to bring
happiness; these hang in the sacred place opposite the
entrance of the family *ger*.

UNDERWORLD OR LOWER WORLD

IN SHAMANIST COSMOLOGY, the Underworld or Lower World forms part of the tripartite universe, which the shaman navigates in company with Spirit help. In classic shamanism, the three worlds—Upper, Middle (this physical world in which we live), and Lower—have to be in balance with one another for life to function properly. As with the universal tree with its branches, trunk, and roots representing these three planes or levels of existence, the three worlds formed necessary parts of a whole. With the introduction of Christianity, however, the Lower World became hell and the abode of the devil.

SEE ALSO: **AXIS MUNDI; BALANCE, HARMONY; CHRISTIANITY**

UPPER WORLD

THE UPPER WORLD, sometimes called the Sky World, forms part of the shamanic tripartite universe. All three worlds—Upper, Middle, Lower—are kept in balance or harmony by shamans. Some cultures—the Hmong of Southeast Asia, for example—see the Upper World as the abode of the ancestors, but as multiples of three; for them, there are nine levels in the Upper World.

WESTERN ALLOPATHIC MEDICINE

IN MANY PARTS of the world, allopathic medicine continues to discredit shamanism as superstitious and nonscientific. In other contexts, however, allopathic medicine and shamanism are blending to produce a syncretic form of medicine that takes into account the physical as well as the spiritual causes of disease and illness. Shamanism is undergoing a revival in places where it has been repressed or even eliminated. Dr. Alexandra

Konstantinova Chirkova in Siberia is an example of a Western-trained physician who draws on her shamanic heritage.

Dr. Alexandra Konstantinova Chirkova and I met in the summer of 2000 at the Ethnomusicology of Tungus-Manchurian Peoples International Conference organized through the Ministry of Culture of the Sakha Republic of the new Russian Federation. The conference was held in Yakutsk City. Dr. Chirkova, from Yakutsk City, is a surgeon and a psychotherapist—a medical doctor trained in Western medicine—who works with ethnic medicine and is associated with the Centre for Traditional Healing.

Could we discuss shamanism with her? I asked. "People are afraid of shamanism," she responded. "Still, even today, they are afraid of the word 'shaman.' Even the word; they are afraid of the word." This fear seems to come from the severe Russian suppression of shamans combined with remembrance of the great power of many Yakutia shamans. Dr. Chirkova is the daughter of the shaman Konstantin (1879–1974). Her father was well known here, she said, but he was considered an enemy of the state. Humiliated and forbidden to practice once Soviet power was established in Siberia, he had all of his shamanic things confiscated. All their family, she said, was oppressed by the Soviet regime—some were put to death. As of the 1920s, shamanism had been officially banned in Siberia by the Communists. Along with confiscation of their belongings by the Soviet authorities, they were forbidden from performing their rites in public. Without the guidance and authority of spiritual leaders, political, economic, and social takeover by the Russians was much easier in Siberia.

Partway through her story, Alexandra brought out herbs from the cabinet behind her to burn in memory of her father. Into a small metal dish, she dropped some twigs and lit them and then "fed the fire" with loose tea grains. "When speaking about my father, we should feed the fire," she said. "Everybody must feed the fire because perhaps he is listening to us." As each of us added a few grains to the dish, she asked whether we had heard the ding-dong of the doorbell earlier. "No one was there," she explained. "It was my father coming here letting me know of his presence. I feel him all the time, and I smudge with these plants to be accompanied by the good spirit of my father."

At school, she had wanted to be a dancer, but her father told her no, that it was not a good profession long-term. She must become a doctor. Alexandra said how much she wanted to be like him, but he said to her, "'I don't want you to repeat my life, my fate.' But he also told me the time will come when the interest comes back in our culture."[181]

X-RAY VISION

X-RAY VISION ENABLES the shaman to see through the veils of reality at the essence of things—a person or animal, a tree, a landscape. It strips away the layers to reveal skeletal and other internal features to the seer.

The X-ray style of art developed early on in human history; Joseph Campbell describes it as characteristic of Paleolithic times and related to the great herds on which early hunting cultures relied. Retreat of the glaciers and the warming of the climate led to the transformation of the tundra to grasslands and then forests in what is now Europe. Seeking new forage, herd animals such as elk, reindeer, and mammoths began their migration northward and eastward, followed by the hunters and eventually crossing the Bering Sea land bridge into what is now North America.[182] This art style, associated with shamanism, is characteristic of the Great Hunt characterized by its mythologies and rituals and its west-to- east dispersal from Eurasia to the Arctic and into North America as well as through India and Australia.[183] Campbell points out the occasional accent of this X-ray style of art as: "the 'lifeline' leading from the animal's mouth or neck to its heart, stomach, or lung," which is especially prominent in the arts of certain areas of North America.[184]

SEE ALSO: **CAMPBELL, JOSEPH; SKELETON MOTIF**

ZOROASTRIANISM

ZOROASTRIANISM IS THE religion of the followers of its prophet and founder, Zoroaster. It is pre-Islamic and one of the world's oldest continuously practiced religions. There is disagreement about its founding dates, but Zoroaster was active in the first millennium BCE in ancient Iran. Today, while Iran and India are its main strongholds, migrations have established communities in North America, Europe, and Australia. A primary aspect of Zoroastrian cosmology is dualism: Two primeval powers or spirits in the universe—good and evil—act out their conflict in this world. Zoroaster also conceived of two kinds of existence and consequently two worlds—the spiritual and the corporeal.[185]

Zoroastrianism is mentioned here because it retains these and other shamanist aspects, but like other religions, its origins are now controversial. Mircea Eliade credited its shamanic past,[186] while Touraj Daryaee presents the idea that "the word Shaman itself appears to be connected with the Zoroastrian tradition, where its origin is assigned to eastern Iran/Central Asia, from the Sogdian language."[187] In Sanskrit, the word appears as *sramana,* and in Middle Persian and Modern Persian appears as *shaman* when it entered into Siberia.[188] Zoroastrianism also includes the concept of the shamanistic voyage,[189] though Daryaee points out that study of a shamanist tradition has caused outrage among modern Zoroastrians, with some scholars denouncing any connection.[190]

SEE ALSO: **ELIADE, MIRCEA; SHAMAN—DEFINITION AND MEANING**

NOTES

1 Marilyn Walker, "New Directions in Shamanic Studies," *The Northern Review: A Multi-Disciplinary Journal of the Arts and Social Sciences of the North*, no. 22 (Winter 2000): 200–203.

2 Michael Harner, *The Way of the Shaman*, Tenth Anniversary Edition. (San Francisco: HarperSanFrancisco, 1990), xx.

3 Knud Rasmussen, *Intellectual Culture of the Hudson Bay Eskimos* [sic], trans. W. J. Alexander Worster and W. E. Calvert (Copenhagen: Gyldendal, 1930), 50–51.

4 Josef Haekel, "Totemism (Religion)," *Encyclopedia Britannica*, last modified May 17, 2019, www.britannica.com/topic /totemism-religion.

5 Joseph Campbell, *The Way of the Animal Powers: Historical Atlas of World Mythology* (London: Times Books Ltd, 1984), 135.

6 Aboriginal Art & Culture, accessed November 20, 2019, aboriginalart.com.au.

7 Luis Eduardo Luna and Pablo Amaringo, *Ayahuasca Visions: The Religious Iconography of a Peruvian Shaman* (Berkeley, CA: North Atlantic Books, 1999), 10.

8 Ibid., 21.

9 Marilyn Walker, "'Oh! You Mean You Have No Balance!' Symmetry, Science and Shamanism," *Shamanhood and Mythology: Archaic Techniques of Ecstasy and Current Techniques of Research*, ed. Attila Mátéffy and György Szabados (Budapest: Hungarian Association for the Academic Study of Religions, 2017), 447–462.

10 Conversation at the 2000 Musical Ethnography of Tungus-Manchurian Peoples conference held in Yakutsk, Republic of Sakha.

11 Marilyn Walker, "Udegei Shamans in the Russian Far East," *The Shamanism Annual* 21 (December 2008): 8–12.

12 Mircea Eliade, *Rites and Symbols of Initiation: The Mysteries of Birth and Rebirth* (New York: Harper & Row, 1958), 101.

13 Geoffrey Samuel, *Civilized Shamans: Buddhism in Tibetan Societies* (Washington, DC: Smithsonian Institution, 1993).

14 Joseph Campbell, *The Power of Myth* (New York: Anchor Books, 1991), 123.

15 Caitlin Matthews, *The Celtic Tradition* (Dorset, UK: Element Books, Ltd, 1995), 40.

16 Caitlin and John Matthews, *Encyclopedia of Celtic Wisdom: A Celtic Shaman's Sourcebook* (Dorset, UK: Element Books Ltd, 1994).

17 Tom Cowan, *Fire in the Head: Shamanism and the Celtic Spirit* (San Francisco: HarperSanFrancisco, 1993).

18 Zhang Weiwen and Zang Qingnan, *In Search of China's Minorities* (Beijing: New World Press, 1993).

19 Fr. Gabriele Amorth, *An Exorcist Tells His Story* (San Francisco: Ignatius Press, 1999).

20 William Friedkin, "The Devil and Father Amorth: Witnessing 'the Vatican Exorcist' at Work," *Vanity Fair*, October 31, 2016.

21 Anatolii Kamenskii, *Tlingit Indians of Alaska*, trans. Sergei Kan, Rasmuson Library Historical Translation Series Vol. 2, ed. Martin W. Falk (Fairbanks: The University of Alaska Press, 1985).

22 As in the Danish-Canadian film *The Journals of Knud Rasmussen* (2006).

23 Michael Harner, personal communication with the author.

24 Carlos Castaneda, *The Teachings of Don Juan: A Yaqui Way of Knowledge* (New York: Ballantine Books, 1968).

25 Michael Harner, "Science, Spirits and Core Shamanism," *Shamanism: Journal of the Foundation for Shamanic Studies* (Spring/Summer 1999): 5–8.

26 Ibid., 7.

27 Mircea Eliade, *Shamanism: Archaic Techniques of Ecstasy*, trans. Willard R. Trask (London: Routledge & Kegan Paul, 1963).

28 John A. Grim, *The Shaman: Patterns of Religious Healing Among the Ojibway Indians* (Norman, OK: University of Oklahoma, 1983).

29 Luna and Amaringo, *Ayahuasca Visions*.

30 Harner, *The Way of the Shaman*, 112.

31 Campbell, *The Way of the Animal Powers*, 169. Drawing from Spencer and Gillen.

32 Eliade, *Rites and Symbols of Initiation*, 97.

33 Claire Dennard, "Archaeology and the Sacred" (unpublished paper given at Interactions with the Sacred Conference, Edinburgh, June 20, 2009).

34 Ellen Pearlman, *Tibetan Sacred Dance: A Journey into the Religious and Folk Traditions* (Rochester, VT: Inner Traditions, 2002).

35 Ibid.

36 Rasmussen, *Intellectual Culture of the Hudson Bay Eskimos*, 57–59.

37 Kathleen Berrin, *Art of the Huichol Indians* (New York: Harry N. Abrams, Inc., 1978).

38 Marilyn Walker, "Shamanism and Traditional Plant Knowledge in Mongolia," *Arctic Studies Center Newsletter*, National Museum of Natural History, Smithsonian Institution, no. 14 (February 2007): 44–45.

39 Eric A. Powell, "Mysterious Mongolia," *Archaeology* 59, no. 1 (January/February 2006), archive.archaeology.org/0601/abstracts/mongolia.html.

40 Campbell, *The Way of the Animal Powers*, 158.

41 Felicitas Goodman, *Where the Spirits Ride the Wind* (Bloomington, IN: Indiana University Press, 1990), 89–90.

42 Marilyn Walker, unpublished field notes, 2000.

43 Melinda C. Maxfield, "Effects of Rhythmic Drumming on EEG and Subjective Experience" (PhD

diss., Institute of Transpersonal Psychology, 1990).

44 Ibid.

45 Nicholas Breeze Wood, "Shaman's Face Masks of Siberia," *Sacred Hoop: The Shamanism Magazine*, issue 80, 2013.

46 Michael Harner, personal communication with the author, 2000.

47 Sónia Silva, "Art and Fetish in the Anthropology Museum," *Material Religion* 3, no. 1 (March 6, 2017): 77–96, doi.org/10.1080/17432200.2016.1272782.

48 Eliade, *Rites and Symbols of Initiation*, 85–86.

49 Peter L. MacNair, "Kwakiutl Winter Dances: A Reenactment," *Arts-canada* (December 1973/January 1974): 98.

50 Bill Holm, "Kwakiutl: Winter Ceremonies," *Handbook of North American Indians* 7 (Washington, DC: Smithsonian Institution, 1990), 378–386.

51 Edward F. Anderson, *Plants and People of the Golden Triangle: Ethnobotany of the Hill Tribes of Northern Thailand* (Portland, OR: Dioscorides Press, 1993).

52 Ibid., 171.

53 Siva Kumar, "What Are Shamans in India Called, and Where Do They Live in South India?," *Quora*, October 2, 2017, quora.com /What-are-shamans-in-India-called-and-where-do-they-live-in-South-India.

54 United Nations, *The United Nations Declaration on the Rights of Indigenous Peoples*, September 13, 2007, un.org/development/desa /indigenouspeoples/declaration -on-the-rights-of-indigenous-peoples.html.

55 Eliade, *Rites and Symbols of Initiation*, 87.

56 Juha Pentikäinen, *Shamanism and Culture* (Helsinki: Etnika Co., 1998), 8.

57 Eliade, *Rites and Symbols of Initiation*.

58 Stanley Krippner, "Anyone Who Dreams Partakes in Shamanism" (Paper presented as a keynote address, Annual Convention of the International Association for the Study of Dreams, Chicago, June 26–28, 2009).

59 José Luis Stevens, *Awaken the Inner Shaman: A Guide to the Power Path of the Heart* (Boulder, CO: Sounds True, 2014).

60 Frank J. Korom, "Of Shamans and Sufis: An Account of a 'Magico-Religious' Muslim Mystic's Career," *Shamanism and Pentecostalism in Asia*, ed. P. Swanson (Nagoya, Japan: Nanzan Institute for Religion and Culture, 2013), 147–169.

61 Thierry Zarcone and Angela Hobart, eds., *Shamanism and Islam: Sufism, Healing Rituals and Spirits in the Muslim World* (London and New York: I.B. Tauri: London, 2017), 154.

62 Campbell, *The Way of the Animal Powers*, 159.

63 Luna and Amaringo, *Ayahuasca Visions*.

64 Gershon Winkler, *Magic of the Ordinary: Recovering the Shamanic in Judaism* (Berkeley, CA: North Atlantic Books, 2003).

65 Celia Rothenberg, "New Age Jews: Jewish Shamanism and Jewish Yoga," *Jewish Culture and History* 8, no. 3 (2006), doi.org/10.1080/14 62169X.2006.10512055.

66 Carl Jung, *Man and His Symbols* (New York: Doubleday & Co., 1964), 151.

67 Luna and Amaringo, *Ayahuasca Visions.*

68 Surenda Bahadur, Christian Rätsch, and Claudia Müller-Ebeling, *Shamanism and Tantra in the Himalayas* (Rochester: Inner Traditions, 2002).

69 Pearlman, *Tibetan Sacred Dance.*

70 Jennifer Ouellette, "A Math Theory for Why People Hallucinate," *Quanta Magazine*, July 30, 2018, quantamagazine.org/a-math-theory-for-why-people-hallucinate-20180730/.

71 Marilyn Walker, "Music as Knowledge in Shamanism and Other Healing Traditions of Siberia," *Arctic Anthropology* 40, no. 2 (2003): 40–48.

72 From author's field notes, 2009.

73 Purev Otgony and Purvee Gurbadaryan, *Mongolian Shamanism: Revised and Updated Fourth Edition* (Ulaanbaatar: Authors Unlimited, 2005).

74 Ibid., 21.

75 Gloria Flaherty, *Shamanism and the Eighteenth Century* (Princeton: Princeton University Press, 1992), 161.

76 Ibid., 163.

77 Ibid.

78 Walker, "Music as Knowledge in Shamanism and Other Healing Traditions of Siberia," 40–48.

79 Daniel J. Levitin, *This Is Your Brain on Music: The Science of a Human Obsession* (New York: Plume, 2006).

80 Robert Jourdain, *Music, the Brain, and Ecstasy: How Music Captures Our Imagination* (New York: William Morrow, 1997).

81 Nikolay Oorzhak. personal communication with the author, 2004.

82 Don G. Campbell, "Music of the Spheres: Ancient Instruments, Modern Vessels," *Quest* 4, no. 3 (Autumn 1991): 88. Unpublished notes.

83 Campbell, *The Way of the Animal Powers.*

84 Campbell, *The Power of Myth*, 27.

85 Ibid., 66.

86 Pentikäinen, *Shamanism and Culture.*

87 Campbell, *The Power of Myth*, 2.

88 Pieter F. Craffert, "Making Sense of Near-Death Experience Research: Circumstance Specific Alterations of Consciousness," *Anthropology of Consciousness* 30, no. 1 (March 2019): 64–89.

89 J. Timothy Green, "The Near-Death Experience as a Shamanic Initiation: A Case Study," *Journal of Near-Death Studies* 19, no. 4 (June 2001): 209–225, doi.org/10.1023/A:1007859024038.

90 Joan B. Townsend, "Western Contemporary Core and Neo-Shamanism and the Interpenetration with Indigenous Societies," *Proceedings of the International Congress Shamanism and Other Indigenous Spiritual Beliefs and Practices* 5, part 1 (1999): 223–31.

91 Pentikäinen, *Shamanism and Culture*, 126.

92 Valentina Kharitonova, "Siberian Field Symposium," *Shamanism* 15, no. 2 (Fall/Winter 2002).

93 Leah Crane, "A Classic Quantum Theorem May Prove There Are Many Parallel Universes," *New Scientist*, August 19, 2019, newscientist.com/article/2213756-a-classic

-quantum-thom-may-prove-there
-are-many-parallel-universes
/#ixzz61WNK6gIl.

94 Larissa MacFarquhar, "The Mind-
Expanding Ideas of Andy Clark,"
New Yorker, April 2, 2018, 62–73.

95 Ibid.

96 Jennifer Ouellette. "A Math Theory
for Why People Hallucinate,"
Quanta Magazine, July 30, 2018,
quantamagazine.org/a-math
-theory-for-why-people
-hallucinate-20180730/.

97 MacFarquhar, "The Mind-Expanding
Ideas of Andy Clark."

98 Jordana Cepelewicz, "Is Consciousness Fractal?" *Nautilus*,
May 4, 2017, nautil.us
/issue/47/consciousness
/is-consciousness-fractal.

99 Wayne Suttles, "Introduction," *Handbook of North American Indians*
7 (Washington, DC: Smithsonian
Institution, 1990), 1–15.

100 Deborah Waite, "Kwakiutl Trans-
formation Masks," *The Many
Faces of Primitive Art: A Critical
Anthology*, ed. Douglas Fraser
(Englewood Cliffs: Prentice-Hall,
1966), 266–300.

101 Joan M. Vastokas, "The Shamanic
Tree of Life," *Artscanada*
(December 1973/January 1974):
125–49.

102 Wayne Suttles and Aldona Jonaitis,
"History of Research in Eth-
nology," *Handbook of North
American Indians* 7 (Washington,
DC: Smithsonian Institution,
1990), 73–87.

103 Niel Gunson, "A Note on Oceanic
Shamanism," *The Journal of
the Polynesian Society* 119, no. 2
(June 2010): 205–212, jstor.org
/stable/20790140.

104 Keith Basso, *Wisdom Sits in Places:
Landscape and Language Among
the Western Apache* (Albu-
querque, NM: University of New
Mexico Press, 1996).

105 Eliade, *Rites and Symbols of
Initiation*.

106 Campbell, *The Way of the Animal
Powers*, 156.

107 Eman M. Elshaikh, "Paleolithic Tech-
nology, Culture, and Art," Khan
Academy, accessed November 21,
2019, khanacademy.org
/humanities/world-history
/world-history-beginnings
/origin-humans-early-societies
/a/paleolithic-culture-and
-technology.

108 Songwit Chuamsakul, "Education
and Hmong Culture Changes: A
Study of Two Hmong Villages in
Northern Thailand" (PhD diss.,
Trent University, June 2006).

109 Walker, "Shamanism and Traditional
Plant Knowledge in Mongolia,"
44–45.

110 Chulu, June 18, 2006.

111 Pentikäinen, *Shamanism and
Culture*, 44.

112 Felicitas D. Goodman, *Where the
Spirits Ride the Wind: Trance
Journeys and Other Ecstatic
Experiences* (Bloomington:
Indiana University Press, 1990).

113 Harner, *The Way of the Shaman*, 65.

114 Ibid.

115 Jim Goodman, *Meet the Akhas*
(Bangkok: White Lotus Co., 1996).

116 Bruce Durie, "Senses Special: Doors
of Perception," *New Scientist*, Jan-
uary 26, 2005, newscientist.com
/article/mg18524841-600
-senses-special-doors-of
-perception/#ixzz61PlCwrDt.

117 Michael Harner, personal communication with the author, 2003.

118 Manohla Dargis, "Herzog Finds His Inner Cave Man," *New York Times,* April 28, 2011.

119 Liz and Peter Welsh, *Rock-Art of the Southwest: A Visitor's Companion* (Birmingham, AL: Wilderness Press, 2004), 48.

120 Eliade, *Rites and Symbols of Initiation,* x.

121 Walker, "'Oh! You Mean You Have No Balance!' Symmetry, Science and Shamanism,", 447–62.

122 Pentikäinen, *Shamanism and Culture,* 11.

123 Ibid., 12.

124 Ibid., 39–40.

125 Äke Hultkrantz, "Introductory Remarks on the Study of Shamanism," *Shaman* 1 (Spring 1993), 7.

126 Sheila Coulson, "World's Oldest Ritual Discovered. Worshipped the Python 70,000 Years Ago (Report)," *Apollon Research Magazine,* February 12, 2012.

127 Spencer Wells, *The Journey of Man: A Genetic Odyssey* (Princeton: Princeton University Press, 2002).

128 Bradford Keeney, *The Bushman Way of Tracking God: The First People Reveal the Original Ways of Healing, Transformation, and Finding the Meaning of Life* (New York: Atria Books, 2010), 269.

129 Bradford Keeney, *Shaking Medicine: The Healing Power of Ecstatic Movement* (Rochester, VT: Destiny Books, 2007).

130 Drew Lopenzina, "Le Jeune Dreams of Moose: Altered States among the Montagnais in the 'Jesuit Relations' of 1634," *Early American Studies* 13, no. 1 (Winter 2015): 3–37, jstor.org /stable/24474903.

131 René R. Gadacz, "Shaking Tent," *Canadian Encyclopedia,* last modified October 20, 2014, thecanadianencyclopedia.ca /en/article/shaking-tent.

132 "Tipatshimuna Collections," *Virtual Museum Canada,* accessed November 21, 2019, tipatshimuna.ca/1110_e .php?catalogue_no=pm25.

133 Campbell (2004), 157.

134 Ibid., 156.

135 Walker, "New Directions in Shamanic Studies."

136 Pentikäinen, *Shamanism and Culture,* 61.

137 Ibid., 60.

138 Sandra Ingerman, *Soul Retrieval: Mending the Fragmented Self* (San Francisco: HarperSanFrancisco, 1991).

139 Stanislav Grof, *The Cosmic Game: Explorations of the Frontiers of Human Consciousness* (Albany, NY: State University of New York Press, 1998).

140 Keeney, *Shaking Medicine.*

141 Eliade, *Rites and Symbols of Initiation,* 14–15.

142 Campbell (2004), 156.

143 Marilyn Walker, "The Drum Is My Ride: Shamans' Drums in Siberian and Mongolia," *Golden Ratio* 1, no. 1 (Spring Equinox 2012), 28–29.

144 David Crockett Graham, *Songs and Stories of the Ch'uan Miao* (Washington, DC: Smithsonian Institution, 1954).

145 Rasmussen, *Intellectual Culture of the Hudson Bay Eskimos,* 50–51.

146 Luna and Amaringo, *Ayahuasca Visions,* 136–7.

147 Sachiko Tamashige, "Seeing Where Shinto and Buddhism Cross," *Japan Times*, May 16, 2013, japantimes.co.jp/culture/2013 /05/16/arts/seeing-where-shinto -and-buddhism-cross/#.XdbC -DJKjBI.

148 Ibid.

149 Dmitriy Funk and Leonard Sillanpää, eds., *The Small Indigenous Nations of Northern Russia: A Guide for Researchers* (Turku: Äbo Akademi University, 1999).

150 Walker, "Music as Knowledge in Shamanism and Other Healing Traditions of Siberia," 40–48.

151 Marilyn Walker, "Integrating Medicines in Sakha: Alexandra Chirkova, Medical Doctor and Shaman's Daughter," *Shamanism, Journal of the Foundation for Shamanic Studies* 18, nos. 1–2 (2005; reprint of 2004 article).

152 Marjorie Balzer and Marjorie Mandelstam, "Soviet Superpowers," *Natural History* 106, no. 2 (March 1997): 38–39.

153 Mihály Hoppál and Keith D. Howard, eds., "Studies on Eurasian Shamanism," *Shamans and Cultures* (Budapest: Korrekt Ltd., 1993), 258–88.

154 Kira Van Deusen. "The Voice of the Mountain Spirit: Contemporary Shamanism in Siberia," *Active Voices, the Online Journal of Cultural Survival* (1997), cs.org /cs%20website/LevelFour /LevelFour-VanDeusen.

155 Pentikäinen, *Shamanism and Culture*.

156 Harner, *The Way of the Shaman*.

157 Valentina Gorbatcheva and Marina Federova, *The Peoples of the Great North: Art and Civilisation of Siberia* (New York: Parkstone Press, 2000).

158 Pentikäinen, *Shamanism and Culture*.

159 Marilyn Walker, "The Spiritual Function of Language" (Paper presentation, Ethnomusicology of Tungus-Manchurian Peoples International Conference, Ministry of Culture of the Sakha Republic, Yakutsk City, Siberia, 2000).

160 Valentina Kharitonova, "Siberian Field Symposium," *Shamanism* 15, no. 2 (Fall/Winter 2002).

161 Luna and Amaringo, *Ayahuasca Visions*.

162 Pearlman, *Tibetan Sacred Dance*, 35.

163 Chuamsakul, "Education and Hmong Culture Changes."

164 Luna and Amaringo, *Ayahuasca Visions*.

165 Angelika Gebhart-Sayer, "The Geometric Designs of the Shipibo-Conibo in Ritual Context," *Journal of Latin-American Lore* 11, no. 2 (1985): 143–75.

166 Diamond Jenness, *The Copper Eskimos, Southern Party, 1913– 1916. Report of the Canadian Arctic Expedition, 1913–1916* (Ottawa: F.A. Acland).

167 Harner, *The Way of the Shaman*.

168 Chuamsakul, "Education and Hmong Culture Changes," 101.

169 Walker, "Music as Knowledge in Shamanism and Other Healing Traditions of Siberia," 40–48.

170 Rasmussen, *Intellectual Culture of the Hudson Bay Eskimos*, 50–51.

171 Marilyn Walker, "More than One Hundred Flowers: An Interview with Anai, a Tsaatan Shaman."

Journal of Shamanic Practice 1 (February 2008): 26–32.

172 Unpublished notes from the Proceedings of the International Interdisciplinary Scientific and Practical Congress, "Sacral Through the Eyes of the 'Lay' and the 'Initiated,'" *Ethnological Studies of Shamanism and Other Indigenous Spiritual Beliefs and Practices* 10, parts 1 and 2 (Moscow, June 21–30, 2004).

173 William R. Seaburg and Jay Miller, "Tillamook," *Handbook of North American Indians* 7 (Washington, DC: Smithsonian Institution, 1990), 560–67.

174 From the website of the Chicago Film Archives, chicagofilmarchives.org /current-events/out-of-the-vault-2012-the-spirit-of-america.

175 David B. Gray, "Hinduism, Rituals, Practices, and Symbolism"; "Buddhism, Practices, Applications, and Concepts," *Oxford Research Encyclopedias*, April 2016.

176 Surendra Bahadur Shahi, Christian Rätsch, and Claudia Müller-Ebeling, *Shamanism and Tantra in the Himalayas* (Rochester, VT: Inner Traditions, 2002), viii.

177 Ibid.

178 Ibid.

179 Samuel, *Civilized Shamans*, 8.

180 Ibid.

181 Marilyn Walker, "The Reindeer Herders of Northern Mongolia: Community, Ecology and Spirit Matters," *Communities* (Summer 2009): 34–39.

182 Walker, "Integrating Medicines in Sakha."

183 Campbell, *The Way of the Animal Powers*, 132.

184 Ibid.

185 Ibid., 133.

186 "Zoroastrianism," *Macmillan Encyclopedia of Death and Dying*, accessed August 1, 2019, encyclopedia.com /social-sciences/encyclopedias -almanacs-transcripts-and-maps /zoroastrianism.

187 Eliade, Shamanism: *Archaic Techniques of Ecstasy*.

188 Ilya Gershevitch, *The Avestan Hymns to Mithra* (Cambridge, UK: Cambridge University Press, 1959).

189 J. R. Russell, "Kartir and Mani: A Shamanistic Model of Their Conflict," *Iranica Varia: Papers in Honour of Professor Eshan Yarshater* (Leiden, Netherlands: Brill, 1990): 180–93.

190 Daryaee Touraj, "Shamanistic Elements in Zoroastrianism: The Pagan Past and Modern Reactions," *Pomegranate* 13 (2000): 31–37.

INDEX

ACKNOWLEDGMENTS

To those who took me into their homes and looked
after my well-being, sometimes in difficult circumstances,
I am so very grateful.

ABOUT THE AUTHOR

Author Marilyn Walker riding a reindeer in Mongolia.

Marilyn Walker, PhD, started out as an archaeologist working in the Canadian North and then became
involved in heritage preservation and museum curatorial
work in the Arctic and Subarctic regions across Canada.
As a university professor of anthropology, her special-
ization in Indigenous studies, medical anthropology, and
ethnobotany involved fieldwork across Canada and the
United States and in Siberia, Mongolia, Southeast Asia,
and India.

Her explorations in shamanism have been personal
as well as academic. She completed Michael Harner's
three-year program of the Foundation for Shamanic
Studies and was invited to become a field associate with
the Foundation for Southeast Asia, Siberia, and northern
North America. A founding member of the Society for
Shamanic Practitioners and a past member of the Society
for the Anthropology of Religion and the Explorers' Club,

she has given papers and workshops nationally and internationally and authored scholarly and popular articles on shamanism along with two books on ethnobotany. Her fieldwork, research, teaching, and publications on Indigenous cultures, shamanism, and ethnobotany have been supported by the Russian Academy of Sciences, the Smithsonian Institution, the National Museums of Canada, the Royal Ontario Museum, and the Social Sciences and Humanities Research Council of Canada as well as national and international educational institutions and funding agencies. Selected publications, some quoted from here, are available online. She is especially interested in the benefits of traditional shamanism for addressing personal and societal problems today and in supporting shamans around the world who have suffered so much repression but are now experiencing a renaissance.

Dr. Walker is now professor emeritus of Mount Allison University in Canada. She retired to her forest garden on Salt Spring Island, British Columbia, where she has a shamanic counseling practice and offers workshops on shamanism, energy medicine, reiki, and other alternative modalities. She is also an artist and singer-songwriter who records and performs as Em Walker.